WHY GREAT LEADERS ARE CATALYSTS

WHY GREAT LEADERS ARE CATALYSTS

Penny du Toit
&
Dr Rowan van Dyk

for

Diana

&

Marietjie

Why Great Leaders are Catalysts
Published by
Penny du Toit & Rowan van Dyk

Wavecrest Leadership Centre,
PO Box 1772,
Swakopmund,
Erongo 9000
Namibia
 www.wave-crest.com

Ordering Information:
Quantity sales. Special discounts are available on quantity purchases by corporations, associations, and others. For details, contact the publisher at the address above.

Printed in Namibia by City Press, Walvis Bay

ISBN:978-99945-85-30-4

First Edition

14 13 12 11 10 / 10 9 8 7 6 5 4 3 2 1

Editing, formatting and design done by
Scribing Dynamics Publishing

Contents

THIS BOOK BELONGS TO:

THIS BOOK WAS GIVEN BY:

MY CURRENT SITUATION:

PREFACE

For more than a century the debate has been raging on whether great leaders are born or whether they are made. The purpose of this book is not to enter into that debate and attempt to establish an answer, instead the book is aimed at creating an awareness that leaders need to act as catalysts. The approach of this book is to highlight the fact that all of us at certain times in our lives need to be leaders, whether we choose to or not. Whenever you are placed in a situation where you become responsible for someone else's actions, or you have someone that needs to report back to you, you are placed in a leadership role.

A mother wants to be a leader for her children, although she has no ambition to become the next president, she wants to be there to show her children the right way and to do her very best to ensure they avoid the dangerous pitfalls in life. A father wants to be a leader for his family because he wants to set the example for his children and build a legacy for himself, his children and the generations to follow.

As we move our way through this complex pathway called life, we display different ambitions at different times. A wife may not specifically want to lead a team, yet she is in charge of the household and needs to lead in areas that concern the specifics that involves running a household. She may not be a born leader, but her instinct requires that she take charge of the situation. You might argue that there are those people who have no inclination to lead and have something similar to a **"I don't care,"** attitude, yet you will find a leader amongst them. In all facets of life, you find various degrees of leadership.

This book is not just another one of those millions of books on leadership that has been churned out over the past century, nor do we want to question who is and who isn't a leader. This book is born out of the frustration that we meet people that have climbed the corporate or political ladder and project themselves as leaders, but will never become great leaders, as they have no concept of what it takes to become a catalyst.

Great leaders become catalysts because they become that spark that ignites a fire in the business, religious or political world. You will find religions that have leaders with a small congregation or membership because people follow them, but they will never succeed in their quest because they don't understand the concept of being a catalyst. The same can be said for any organization.

If you want to become a catalyst you need to find that spark, that singular event or message that becomes the trigger for that atomic bomb you are sitting on.

Jesus did not come to earth to tell everybody that would listen to Him about heaven and how beautiful it will be one day. He did not sell a dream. He had one clear message:

John 3:16 For God so loved the world that He gave His only begotten Son, whosoever believeth in Him should not perish, but have everlasting life.

Although that message was driven with passion, it came with some clear reality checks. You had to admit that you were a sinner; you had to repent and turn away from your sins; you had to follow a process of asking forgiveness for your sins committed against your neighbours, friends or family. Nowhere was there any proclamation that it would be a joy-ride or an easy journey, yet people followed Him. A new religion was born called Christianity all because someone was a catalyst. He set the whole world on fire with His message. He had a singular message, but He had to show the way, teach the principles and stand by what He said, even when they crucified Him, the message stayed the same.

In this book, you will not find out if you were born to be a leader or whether you have the attributes and personality to be taught how to be a leader, rather how you can become a Catalyst Leader. In this book, we will take you on a journey and introduce you to the Leadership Flag and why it is essential in developing a Catalyst Leader. This book will show you what a catalyst is. This will lead to the Core of the Cabbage™, a concept of applying the catalyst leadership in your personal and professional career.

This book will have various personal self-evaluation pages where you can evaluate yourself, where you can be honest with yourself and identify your own gaps. This is not a book that you simply just read and work through and then give to a friend afterwards. This is personal and therefore when you get this book, you will find in the first few pages who this book belongs to. Write it down and keep your book for yourself. Don't read this book as a story because it won't work. Don't buy this book if you are not ready to be honest with yourself.

This book will take you on a journey of discovering your hidden message, that message that has driven you from the day you were born. It will take you on a journey where you will realize that the message changes as the years go by, but it will entice you to become a catalyst.

The book has been, merely for practical reasons, divided into three parts and also includes an introduction and a conclusion. Each part can be seen as a separate concept but these are brought together in the conclusion to demonstrate the context. The introduction is to lay the foundation for the book and to emphasise the various thoughts in the marketplace on what leadership is and what the attributes of leaders are based on the thoughts of some of the top business writers.

INTRODUCTION

Leadership is a topic that has been thrown around since any form of structure took place in human history. It is such a widely discussed topic that currently on Amazon.com there are over 1200 books on leadership alone and these are only the books that were published in the last four years. It seems safe to say that this is a popular topic and that there are numerous suggestions as to what makes a good leader.

Well-known authors such as Kenneth Blanchard, Stephen Covey and John C. Maxwell, to name but a few have written many of their own books on the topic but whatever flavour you give these leadership attributes it always boils down to the same five basic key attributes or skills that a true leader requires.

Whether you are comparing the leadership style of Jesus of Nazareth or whether you are looking at someone on the complete opposite end of the spectrum such as Adolph Hitler, whether you consider the most successful business leaders or the local football team captain, the following five attributes, in whichever manner you explain or describe

them, will always surface:
Lead by example

- Be focussed on your goal
- Treat your followers with respect
- Have a solid set of values and beliefs
- Communicate effectively (this includes listening)

In an interview[1] with 100 of the top CEOs in the world regarding what they saw as their secrets for successful leadership, the attributes of a successful leader were identified.

The CEOs included the likes of:

- David McClaughlin – Chairman of the American Red Cross
- Chip Perry – President of AutoTrader.com
- Terdema Ussery – CEO of the Dallas Mavericks
- William Lauder – CEO and President of Estee Lauder
- James Keyes – CEO of 7-Eleven, Inc. Industries

The following are leadership skills or attributes that were identified by these CEOs based on their personal experiences in leading large organisations:

- Surround yourself with successful people
- Treat your employees well and keep them motivated
- Be honest and ethical
- Be flexible and adaptive and embrace change by making it happen
- Guide your people and lead by example
- Communicate with and listen to your people
- Lead your people the way you want to be led
- Allow people to take risks and make mistakes

Many authors and leadership trainers still use Abraham Maslow's hierarchy of needs as the basis to teach skills on motivation, but Maslow wrote his hierarchy of needs 74 years ago and things have changed drastically since then. The hierarchy still applies today but instead of the basic needs of shelter and food people are now more interested in free WiFi.

In essence, the basic context of a hierarchy of needs stills exists, and is very much relevant to today's business world, however there have been changes in the types of needs described by Maslow as society has evolved and we have become more and more entrenched in the technological advances of the 21st Century.

In the same way that societal needs have changed to suit the times, leadership is also adapting. Whereas the basic skills of leadership, and the attributes mentioned earlier still apply, the application of these attributes and the needs of the followers has changed. We are no longer leading Baby Boomers and we now have to deal with a whole new range of expectations from Millennials. So even though the basic attributes still apply today, we have to adapt our thinking to the way we apply these attributes to deal successfully with the upcoming generations that have other priorities than the ones we are accustomed to. If we cannot adapt to a new way of thinking then how will we become the catalyst to lead the next generation or the one after?

Besides having to deal with the new generations entering the market place, of which statistics show us will make up nearly 34%[1] of the total labour force by 2024 in the United States alone, we also have to deal with the mix of people

---

1   US Bureau of Labor Statistics. 2017. Labor force projections to 2024 —- US Bureau of Labor Statistics. [ONLINE] Available at: https://www.bls.gov/opub/mlr/2015/article/labor-force-projections-to-2024-12.htm

with different cultural, spiritual and ethnical backgrounds that are thrown into the melting pot as a result of the global economy that has come into existence over the last few decades. People are being thrown together in the workplace across the globe and they are required to professionally interact with each other on a daily basis. These people also report to their respective leaders who may be stationed on the other side of the globe. These differences can hinder the way the leader effectively leads his followers.

Other aspects that play a major role in the way leaders need to adapt includes the gaps in the salary structures, the way people save or build up nest eggs, the way people view and plan for their future and the emphasis various individuals and groups place on wealth and wealth creation. These factors, when compromised, can create a volatile situation in the workplace and is exactly the type of situation where the modern-day leader can become the catalyst for change.

Prior to the technological advances being made in recent years, people did not have access to the stream of information that is being broadcast over the internet. Potential leaders would be identified and groomed locally and incumbent leaders had to imitate the skills and attributes observed in their local leaders. They may even have had the opportunity to read a book or two about some of the national leaders or have been able to access to information in the print media. These days we have the internet, a tool that is highly sought after by Millennials for gathering information, that provides us with so much information at the push of a button. You can view the blogs, podcasts or YouTube clips of famous world leaders such as the likes of Warren Buffet (American business magnate), Nelson Mandela (first democratically elected president of South Africa), Bill Gates (Founder of Microsoft) to name but a few. The interest is amassed with what we have come to refer to as *Webfluentials*, individuals who through various means including endorsements of people, products or services, or relating stories and accounts of successful leaders and what they have achieved. This creates the ideal opportunity for new leaders to become greater leaders through the availability of this online coaching and teaching. The opportunity now exists for up and coming leaders to be great leaders in their communities, but through the availability of internet access they can now also gain international recognition as a leader.

It is estimated that the average consumer mentions specific brands nearly 100 times a week in conversation with friends or family and that as much as up to 60% of people feel that Facebook is the most trusted platform for product and service recommendations. One of the recognised attributes of a great leader, as cited by many of the authors mentioned previously, is establishing trust amongst your followers. As a prime example, let us investigate the outcome of the 2008 global economic meltdown, and the major impact the actions of the super-heroes of the world economy had on the levels of trust of the rest of the population.

In short, the economic super-powers, especially the United States of America, manipulated the money markets of the world by creating a false sense of economic security, primarily it appears for personal gain, and refused to see or listen to the warning signs from as early as the 1990's. They refused to implement regulation that would regulate the way banks, investment firms and insurance companies did business and this led to the massive economic crash in September 2008 that saw millions and millions of people suddenly jobless and homeless across the globe. This resulted in the world no longer trusting these large conglomerates.

Even though Warren Buffet himself said that investment bankers were not trustworthy and that they were more interested in enriching themselves rather than benefiting their clients' interest, he nevertheless acquired an investment firm, *Salomon Brothers*, which also overstepped the line and were investigated and suspended by the Securities and Exchange Commission (SEC) of the United States of America. At the time, he was heard to remark that "you spend 20 years building a reputation and you can destroy it in five minutes".

He was referring to the broken trust and compromised effectiveness as a leader. Fortunately, Warren Buffet has been a responsible and ethical businessman all his life and this reputation enabled him to convince the SEC to allow Salomon Brothers to start trading again otherwise hundreds of people would have lost their jobs.

Further distrust was caused because the so-called regulators of the economy, or world economy for that matter, were not doing their job, and this resulted in unscrupulous economic dealings going un-checked. We are referring to the three largest rating agencies, namely **Moody's**, **Fitch** and **Standard & Poor**, who were tasked with ensuring that investors knew who the sound companies were and who the shady ones were. These rating agencies were giving AAA ratings to the very companies that were in fact committing worldwide fraud, because it is claimed that they were being paid for issuing certain ratings.

They are still conducting ratings to this day but it appears that they have also lost the trust they once had. A prime example of this would be South Africa, who were given Junk Status but this did not have the desired effect of stemming investment. It seems as though there has been no decline in investment.

Warren Buffet, who ensured that he remained ethical through all his business dealings, could be considered a prime example of a catalyst as he has influenced many great business leaders. He is even highly respected by Bill Gates. His wife Susie Buffet, was also a major catalyst in his life as she managed to get him to become a Democrat, even though he grew up a Republican and his father was a Republican Senator.

She did this through her constant interaction with him and setting the example for him to follow which made him change his views.

WHAT IS A LEADER?

The Merriam-Webster dictionary defines leadership or to lead as "to *guide a way by going in advance*" or "*to direct a course or direction*". The same dictionary defines management as "to *administer or direct*" and "*to make or keep compliant*". A catalyst, according to the dictionary is "*an agent that provokes or speeds significant change or action*".

From these definitions, it appears that both a leader and a manager could be a catalyst for change in the organisation. Later on, in subsequent chapters, we will explain why a manager cannot be a successful catalyst but a true leader can

It therefore stands to reason that the most logical explanation or definition of what leadership is, must be the ability to accomplish a task or set of tasks through others providing their assistance and support. It is argued that a leader does not necessarily have to have power or position to be the leader. It could be assumed that this statement could be argued in many ways depending on how you interpret the concept of power or position.

On one hand, you would need to exercise some form of power, most likely in the form of authority, to get people to follow you, but then again it could be argued that you would require influence rather than power to get people to follow you.

John C. Maxwell[2] suggests that leadership is not a position but a process. He further suggests that there are five levels of leadership that a leader will progress through to become the ultimate leader.

There are many varying opinions on leadership and management and whether they are one and the same. If you agree with the argument put forward in the previous section that you do not need power or position to be a leader then it stands to reason that you would also not need to be a manager to lead. You could be a leader and also be a manager. The difference between a manager and a leader is that:

Managers concentrate on details; and
Leaders concentrate on change (being a catalyst)

Managers plan in detail and then focus primarily on getting the work done according to the plan. Managers focus on creating stability and usually have short-term horizons[3].

Leaders on the other hand tend to set direction and focus more on leading the team in a specific direction. Leaders focus on creating change and this requires long-term horizons.

Frederick Taylor[4] suggested that the primary role of managers was to improve profits. Of the three principles he promoted, the training and up-skilling of employees was one. This was to improve the skills of the employees so that they could do better work and more work in order for the organisation to improve their profits through improved productivity. We can see that as far back as the 1900's authors like Taylor already saw the significance of up-skilling and empowering employees but due to the times they were living in the full impact of building relations with employees had not been grasped yet. The focus was therefore still on managing and getting the job done rather than leading employees. The workers were also not properly compensated for the skills or knowledge of the machine or the job, so they did not perform to their peak and a process similar to a "go-slow" action in today's age was implemented.

Taylor noticed that some workers were more skilled or talented than others, and that even smart ones were often unmotivated. He also noticed that most workers who are forced to perform repetitive tasks tend to work at the slowest rate possible to escape punishment. Taylor used the term "soldiering", a term that reflects the way conscripts may approach following orders. What Taylor also noticed was that, when workers were paid the same wages, they would tend to do the amount of work that the slowest among them does.

Taylor acknowledged that if each employee's compensation was linked to their output, their productivity would go up.

Taylor promoted many attributes through "Taylorism", but the two that stood out were:

Work ethic:
>   It is the value based on hard work and diligence.

> It is commonly believed that there is great benefit in hard work and that it has the ability to enhance a person's character.

Knowledge transfer:

> This refers to sharing or disseminating of knowledge and providing inputs to amongst other aspects, problem solving. Knowledge transfer is the practical problem of transferring knowledge from one part of the organisation to another.

Berson and Stieglitz[5] feel that managers tend to focus more on getting the job done and in the process, tend to forget about leading. Management tends to readily promote the person who is technically the best, or the best consultant or salesperson into the management position thereby perpetuating the cycle of not developing leaders but finding the person who does the job the best.

Unfortunately, in many cases, the person may know how to do the job the best but has no idea of how to get someone else to do the job just as well and therefore fails as a leader.

This is a classic example of the Peter Principle[6] where an employee rises to the height of their own incompetence. The Peter Principle states that the members of an organization where promotion is based on achievement, success, and merit will eventually be promoted beyond their level of ability.

This could be better explained as employees being given increasing authority until they cannot continue to work competently. An example of this would be where the best

performing sales person is promoted to sales manager. They may possess superb selling skills but they do not know how to lead people. Therefore you don't have to be a manager to be a leader - you don't have to have any authority - everyone has the potential to be a manager. [7]
Another dilemma that surfaced was whether or not leaders could be developed or did one have to be born with certain characteristics that made you a leader.

There are three distinct schools of thought:
Great Man Theory – Thomas Carlyle (1840) believed that effective leaders were a package of Godly motivation and the right personality

Trait Leadership Theory – Sir Francis Galton (1869) has been credited with developing this theory that claims you have to be born with certain personality traits to be a good leader, and that these traits cannot be taught

Behavioural Leadership Theory – John Broadus Watson (1913) was the founder of behavioural leadership. He claimed that leaders could be taught by following the example of other great leaders.

These are well documented and we are not endeavouring to re-introduce these theories but merely would like to point out that even though these theories, when developed at their specific time, seem to have become extinct, there are still remnants of the past two evident in the workplace today. We still aspire to be like the great leaders of our time, and we still believe that leaders must possess certain characteristics to be a great leader.

Our argument therefore is to suggest that there are certain

role-models we can shape our leadership skills on and that we can learn the various attributes that make a great leader by modelling our behaviour on others. The process that enables leaders to develop these skills and attributes will now be discussed further.

Even though the three main leadership theories are from different eras and were essentially developed based on differing contexts, all three of them still apply in varying degrees today. Warren Buffet and Bill Gates are philanthropists and give away most of their wealth to charitable institutions, so this would make them great men in the eyes of Carlyle and the world.

However, they are also very successful and effective business leaders who have been a catalyst for many other great and even aspiring leaders. It is also true though that both Warren Buffet and Bill Gates and all the other great leaders have achieved their success through a combination of specific attributes as well as other circumstances in life that assisted them throughout their career.

To name but one example, both Buffet and Einstein had special mathematical abilities that assisted them in their chosen field or occupation.

part 1

THE LEADERSHIP FLAG

WHAT IS THE LEADERSHIP FLAG?

There have been many people, including Warren Buffet, who have used leadership as an acronym and allocated various skills or attributes to the letters of LEADERSHIP.

In our experience however, we differ with some of the attributes that have been attached to the letters and have therefore developed our own acronym for leadership.

Below is a diagram depicting a flag of what we believe how the acronym should look, as well as the detailed explanations and rationale behind each skill or attribute.

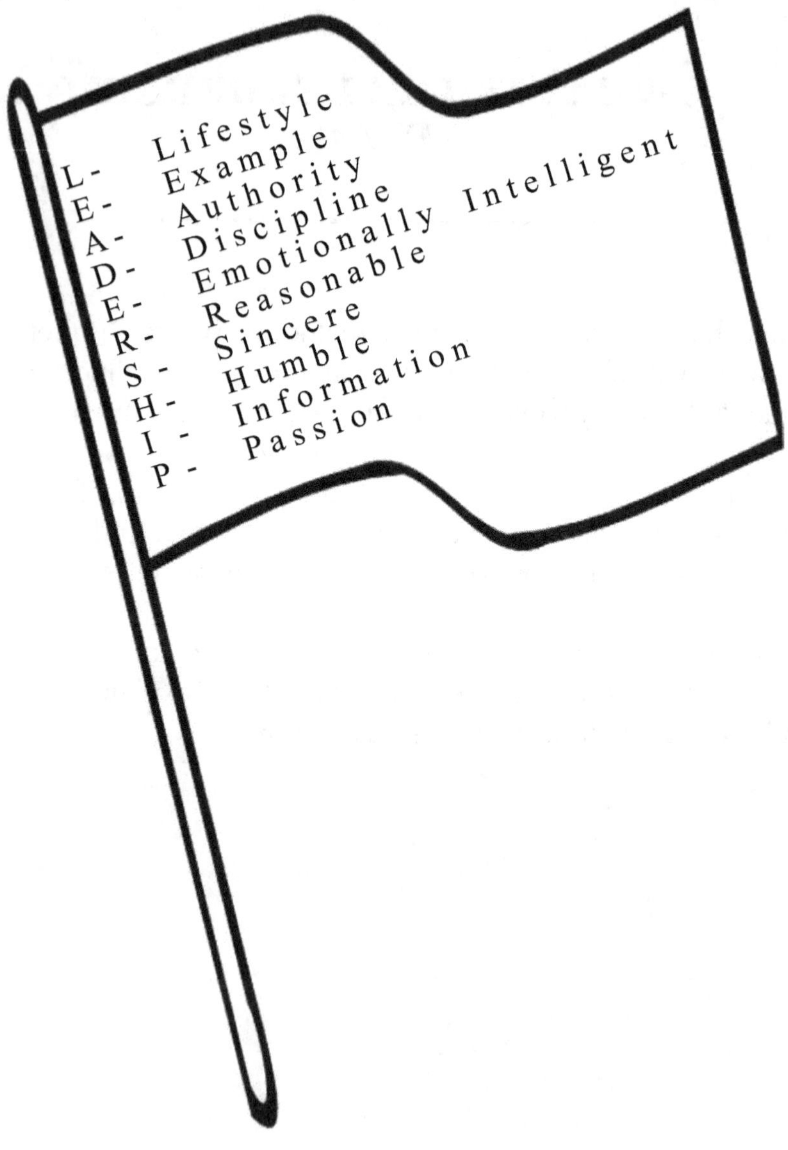

L-   Lifestyle
E-   Example
A-   Authority
D-   Discipline
E-   Emotionally Intelligent
R-   Reasonable
S-   Sincere
H-   Humble
I - Information
P - Passion

We have purposely depicted the acronym as a flag to enable you to fly your flag with pride. In years past, nations and clans used to go to war with the flag, or colours as it was referred to, carried out in front, holding them high for everyone to see. In the same way, you should be proud of your skills and attributes as a great leader and fly your flag so everyone can see.

In the United States of America, they pledge allegiance to their flag. This is a very noble idea that a nation does not bow in respect to a king or emperor, but rather to the flag of the country. Why a flag? A flag represents honour, respect and even victory. For leaders to follow other leaders with a message is great, but ultimately leaders should focus on the flag of leadership that represents the core values that true leaders believe in.

At sea, flags are used to identify merchant ships from hospital ships, and as you may realise, this would often mean the difference between life and death. Flags are also used to display messages of distress as well as a sign of celebration.

At the Wave-Crest Leadership Centre we also employ the use of a flag. Young up-and-coming leaders need something to hold on to. They need direction, mentorship and much more. The Leadership Flag represents victory over adversity for leaders and indicates the values that are required to be successful as leader.

The Leadership Flag is used as the basis for the allegiance of young and emerging leaders that pass through the Wave-Crest Leadership Centre, where the emerging leaders swear allegiance in the form of the Wave-Crest pledge below:

They pledge allegiance to the Leadership Flag as the basis of their values and pledge to live a **L**ifestyle befitting a true leader. They pledge to be an **E**xample for others and to exercise **A**uthority, **D**iscipline and **E**motional-Intelligence as required by a successful leader. They pledge to always act **R**easonably and with **S**incerity and **H**umility towards their followers and team members, and to display the vision by sharing **I**nformation regularly with their team to empower ad develop them. Furthermore, they pledge to **P**assionately live and share the message of their vision in order to achieve the maximum results as a true leader.

Having a great vision or message, and assembling a team to bring that concept to life is the first step in creating a successful business. But while finding new and unique messages is rare enough, the ability to successfully implement the message and take it forward is what separates the sheepdog from the sheep. Henry Ford said, "A vision without execution is merely hallucination."

However, when money is tight, stress levels are high, and when the vision of instant success does not happen like you thought, it is easy to lose your passion, kick into survival mode and bark out instructions in an attempt to resurrect your vision and thereby lose your team. Take a breath, calm yourself down, and remind yourself of the leader you are and would like to become and involve your whole team in the plan and end goal. That way they will know where you are going and will be in a better position to help you get there.

LIFESTYLE

If you want to influence or direct others to achieve an objective, you must be the role-model. You must be aware of:

- How you talk to people
- The way you look or dress
- The company you keep

Our belief is that through observing the behaviour of successful leaders, people can be taught to be successful leaders themselves. Therefore, it is vital that as a leader being observed or imitated, you do not create the wrong impression

As mentioned previously, Warren Buffet said "It takes 20 years to build a reputation and only 5 minutes to ruin it. Think how you will do things differently". People look to you as the leader and also as the role-model. If you stumble they will pick up on it immediately and it will tarnish your reputation as a leader. The lifestyle you live is similar but also distinctly different from the example you set.

If you are a strict disciplinarian type leader at work who enforces the ethics and values of the organisation religiously, but on weekends you are the proverbial party animal and you disregard societal rules in the process, your followers are not going to trust you because of your double standards.

If you, as the leader, are the one always telling the dirty jokes, or you constantly cuss and use foul language in the workplace, or outside the workplace, you will not gain the respect of your followers and achieve the objectives of the company or team will be fruitless.

Use the following **Lifestyle Checklist** to measure your lifestyle as a catalyst leader. Remember to be honest with yourself because you are the only one who sees this and you alone know if you are being honest.

The score you allocate is based on the scale below where
1.   Definitely do not agree
2.   Disagree
3.   Not sure
4.   Agree
5.   Definitely agree

SKILL, ATTRIBUTE, ACTION	1	2	3	4	5
You are mindful of the type of language you use when communicating with others in a business environment					
You live a life that others can follow and that is a positive influence on others					
You dress in a way that you can be respected as a leader					
You talk to others showing respect and consideration towards their feelings					
The people you associate with both professionally and privately will not be an embarrassment in your role as a leader					
Total Score out of 25					

NOTES

EXAMPLE

If you expect your followers to produce the results you desire, you are going to need to lead by example. Nothing motivates a follower more than seeing the boss roll up his sleeves and gets his hands dirty along with all the others in the trenches, showing them that hard work takes place on every level. By proving your commitment to the business and your role as leader, you will earn the respect of your followers and you will also set the work ethic benchmark that will generate the same hard working energy among your followers.

You must be prepared to lead by your example, which is not the same as **Lifestyle**. In order to lead by example, you should not expect your followers to perform tasks you are not prepared to perform yourself. We have established that the difference between a leader and a manager is that a leader "leads the way", so you should be prepared to set the pace; to show the direction; to have the capacity and ability to do what you expect your followers to do.

Carlyle believed that leaders were great men and cited examples of people such as Napoleon Bonaparte, but great military leaders do not lead the charge, they remain behind to strategize. A true leader sets the example and leads from the front.

Another way in which a leader sets the example is, not just by knowing the Vision, Mission and Core Values of the organisation, but by being completely committed to them and living them out in every action and deed. The core values of the organisation determine the culture of the organisation. By enforcing, living and even being the culture, you as the leader will set the correct example for your team to follow.

Your overall attitude should be a positive one. True leaders do not see problems but instead see opportunities. A true leader will use the **S**trengths, **W**eaknesses, **O**pportunities, and **T**hreats identified in a **SWOT** analysis and turn them into opportunities for success.

You want to keep your team motivated towards the continued success of the company, and keep the energy levels up. Whether that means providing snacks, coffee, relationship advice, or even just an occasional beer in the office, remember that everyone on your team is a person. Keep the office mood a fine balance between productivity and playfulness.

If your team is feeling happy and upbeat, chances are they won't mind staying that extra hour to finish a report, or devoting their best work to the brand.

There may be days where the future of your business is uncertain and things aren't going according to plan. This happens with any business, large or small on occasion. The most important thing is to not panic, because it is part of your job as a leader to put out fires and maintain the team morale. Keep up your confidence level, and assure everyone that setbacks are natural and the important thing is to focus on the end goal.

Remember that having a positive attitude is not measured by how happy you are or how much you smile, it is measured by how quickly you bounce back from a negative incident. Your team will be watching you to model their own behaviour, so how quickly you get up and dust yourself off after being knocked down, is going to determine how positive and enthusiastic they will be towards your vision or message. By staying calm and confident, you will help keep the team feeling the same. The ultimate objective is to keep everyone working and moving ahead.

There was a stage where we consulted a manufacturing company that was required to become International Organisation of Standardisation (ISO 9001:2008) accredited to retain their contracts with their large customers. This company embarked on the ISO accreditation process and we consulted and advised on putting the entire Quality Management System and system in place for them. As they had never had ISO accreditation, and this was a family business passed down through the generations that had previously been very active in a different industry, no processes were in place and we had to develop the system from the ground up.

The CEO of the company was aware that the process was needed in order for them to retain their customers, but there was very little support from him with regards to setting up the system.

The implementation and maintenance of the ISO system required that certain practices and procedures be scrapped, implemented or redeveloped in the factory. One of the procedures required the demarcation of areas, designated walking areas, restricted areas for operators only and green areas for production meetings. A job card system was also implemented as part of the ISO process. Another major impact on the factory and the workers in general was that the compulsory wearing of the appropriate Personal Protective Equipment (PPE) and clothing was enforced.

The CEO however set an incorrect example and also poor self-discipline in that he would walk wherever he pleased, and when confronted by the safety representatives he would merely remark that he was the boss and the rules did not apply to him. In time, the staff systematically stopped following the rules and regulations. The same applied to the wearing of PPE where the CEO felt that it was not necessary to wear earplugs and safety shoes when walking through the factory. In time, the rules all went out the window and ultimately, they lost their ISO certification and we were called in to restart the entire process as they had lost some of their major clients.

The poor example set by the CEO through his actions, rubbed off on the rest of the employees and it lost the company serious revenue. They scaled down their operations and retrenched 2/3 of their staff to cope with the financial losses. It took seven months to re-instate their ISO certification and another nine months to show a growth in revenues and the business as a whole

Use the following Example Checklist on the next page to measure the example you set for your followers as a catalyst leader. Remember to be honest with yourself because you are the only one who sees this.

The score you allocate is based on the scale below where

1. Definitely do not agree
2. Disagree
3. Not sure
4. Agree
5. Definitely agree

SKILL, ATTRIBUTE, ACTION	1	2	3	4	5
You are prepared to get your hands dirty and do the jobs you expect your followers to do					
You know what the vision, mission and core values of your organisation are					
You live and communicate the vision, mission and core values daily to your followers					
You display a positive attitude towards your organisation, yourself and your followers					
You set the example by following the rules you enforce yourself					
TOTAL SCORE OUT OF 25					

NOTES

AUTHORITY

Authority could also be described as being assertive. The most important factor that develops your authority as a leader, is trust. Your team however will only trust you if you are truthful with them in all aspects of the business

It is important to not only show your commitment to the work at hand, but also to your promises. If you promised to host an office party, or to implement Casual Fridays, then make sure you keep your word. It is of utmost importance, not only to create the reputation of work ethic, but also to be a fair leader and the catalyst in building trust relations throughout your entire organisation. As soon as you gain the respect of your team, and they trust you as a fair and reliable leader, they will be more likely to deliver peak performances at the highest quality work possible.

- Your word must mean something.
- If you promise to do something, do it
- Are you dependable?
- Can you be trusted?
- Do you keep your word?

Let us illustrate this concept by means of an example from our dealings with various organisations.

In one particular incident with a security company, we experienced the following scenario where a newly appointed manager noticed, in his getting to know the job, that each individual security guard had an entry on their payslip which indicated that they received N$50 "bonus" every month. On enquiring from the General Manager as to the motivation for the bonus, he was informed that it constituted a monthly performance bonus.

On further investigation, the new manager found that the core values, and therefore culture of the company, were encased in the main rules governing the appearance of a security guard. These rules were that male guards had to be clean shaven and were not allowed any form of beard or moustache. Only certain ranks could wear a moustache. Furthermore, their shoes had to be cleaned daily and they had to wear the name badges in plain sight on the uniform. The manager, through personal visits to the guards' sites, discovered that most of the men had some form of beard, and that very few of them wore their proper uniform or had their name badges in sight. They did however receive the bulk of their bonus every month.

Again, he enquired from the General Manager and was informed that should one of the guards have been reported to not be conforming to the rules, they were "punished" by having N$4 deducted from their bonus. The manager then took an executive decision to rectify the situation and went around to every site and spoke personally to each guard in turn, and informed them that going forward, if any guard was found not to be conforming to the rules, their entire bonus for the month would be deducted as it was after all a performance bonus. All the guards willingly agreed to the new arrangement.

The next month not a single guard received their bonus and there was nearly a mutiny and strike action. The manager reminded each one of the guards that he had personally conveyed the new requirements for receiving a performance bonus to them and that they had agreed to the new arrangements. It must also be stated that at that point in time the average monthly salary of a security guard was in the region of N$1500. Needless to say, it was the only month that they lost their monthly performance bonus.

The point of the example is that, had the manager caved in to the pressure and paid the bonus regardless, he would have lost all authority. He had promised them that should the incident occur he would take action. By keeping his word and taking action he showed that he could be trusted.

From a leadership point of view, in the future the guards would know that if he promised certain action, whether positive or negative, he could be trusted to follow through. His authority was never questioned again.

Lines of Authority

Sometime later this same manager was promoted to regional manager in another larger region that also made use of site supervisors. Now he noticed the same thing with the site supervisors, who had to supervise guards at more than one site. Except in this case the supervisors received a monthly performance bonus of N$500. What the manager noticed after the first few months of getting to know the operational processes better, was that there were some of the supervisors who never went to visit the sites, and as they were not being compelled to submit the required monthly site reports, no-one was noticing their lack of operational compliance to standards.

So, the manager decided to implement the same actions he had previously implemented at the site he was stationed before receiving the current promotion. He had a meeting with all the supervisors in his office and explained what was required and the format of the report that was to be submitted monthly. He got the buy-in from all the supervisors that should they fail to submit any of their reports, they would forfeit the entire monthly performance bonus.

At the end of the month he requested the operational assistant to draw all the site visit reports for that month, to his dismay only one supervisor had submitted a daily report for each of the sites visited. The rest had either not submitted any reports or only a few sporadic reports. As in the previous incident he withheld all the performance bonusses for that month for the supervisors, except for the one supervisor who had complied fully with the requirements.

As you can expect there was mayhem and an emergency meeting was requested in his office by all the supervisors. They demanded their bonusses, but the manager informed them that they had all agreed to the arrangement that he would withhold their bonus if they did not submit the site visit reports as required by the operation procedures of the organisation.

If he had not followed through and kept his promise it would compromise his authority. They left his office and marched straight into the executive manager's office to lay out their grievances.

What happened next escalated the situation. The executive manager, without any consultation, paid the managers their bonusses that had been withheld. In one single action, the executive manager broke down the work ethic the manager was trying to establish, which was in fact required by company policies and procedures. Furthermore, the executive manager completely negated the authority of the manager over his supervisor's. It took the manager several months after that to firstly, convince the executive manager to back him in his decisions, and then to get the supervisors to accept his authority. All of this could have been avoided had the executive manager endorsed the authority of his manager and not intervened of his own accord.

A Chain of Command or Hierarchy of Authority, once established must be strictly adhered to. It is similar to a family scenario where the mother continuously warns the children that as soon as the father comes home, they will get a spanking.

The net result is that whenever the mother wants something done or orders the children to do something, they will ignore her as she will not punish them. On the other hand, if the father gives an instruction, they will carry it out immediately because they want to avoid a spanking.

This simple example is critical in the workplace for any leader, because if the authority is not delegated along with the responsibility of the position, chaos will ensue and the leader will be rendered ineffective.

As can be seen from the examples above, trust is key to the success of the authority of a leader. If there is no trust then the outcomes will not be achieved. In the first example, it took only one month to set the new regulations into action because the leader followed through on his promise even when it caused friction. The result was that from the following months the regulations were enforced and the staff adhered to them.

In the second example in the Lines of Authority chapter, it can be seen that the new manager failed to create a working model due to unnecessary interference from senior management. Because of that interference the chain of command was broken and authority was lost.

Use the following Authority Checklist to measure your reliability and consistency as a catalyst leader and how you measure. Remember to be honest with yourself because you are the only one who sees this and you alone know if you are being honest.

The score you allocate is based on the scale below where
1. Definitely do not agree
2. Disagree
3. Not sure
4. Agree
5. Definitely agree

SKILL, ATTRIBUTE, ACTION	1	2	3	4	5
You always do what you said you were going to do					
You follow the lines of authority both up through the line and down and you never side-step anyone in the chain of command					
You are honest in all your dealings with people					
You are reliable and consistent in your decision making					
You can be trusted to stand up for your followers					
TOTAL SCORE OUT OF 25					

NOTES

DISCIPLINE

The difference between good leaders and great leaders often is their discipline. Having a whole range of positive traits does not serve as an excuse for a lack of discipline. Having proper discipline allows leaders more flexibility, but subjecting yourself to the rigour of discipline is not easy, although it is essential if you want to maximize your effectiveness as a leader. The best leaders usually are extremely disciplined people and they simply do the things others are not willing to do. Are you disciplined in all facets of your life, or just those which come more easily to you?

A lot has been said and written about strengths and weaknesses, but "playing to your strengths" is often just an excuse to not do things you dislike or that you don't happen to be very good at. It is far easier for most people to hone their areas of strength and to soak up the admiration for being a high achiever than to be honest about their shortcomings. You don't need to observe a leader for long to know whether or not they're disciplined. Disciplined leaders stand out because they're the ones that get things done, the ones you can count on.

By applying rigorous discipline to all aspects of your personal and professional life that you normally tend to avoid, your strengths will be even more prominent. There is a saying that "Discipline is the refining fire by which talent becomes ability." So why not apply the discipline it takes to ensure that outcome?

Real leaders don't accept mediocrity, they constantly seek improvement. If you want to become a true leader that is noticed as opposed to someone who has great potential, become very intentional about bringing discipline to every area of your life. Take an evaluation of what you do well and what you don't, and then apply rigour, process, structure and discipline to each of those areas. Hard work isn't easy, but it does pay huge dividends

Jocko Willink and Leif Babin[1] bring together their experience as Navy SEALs in the Iraq combat and apply them to leadership. They share examples of field combat and apply them towards leading teams in business. For every topic, they discuss they state a clear principle with an "application to business" that helps you understand how to apply what they are teaching to your leadership.

The overall message of the book addresses the importance of owning the results of what you do. They emphasise the importance of discipline in leadership. "If you have the discipline to get out of bed, you win, you pass the test." According to Willink, waking up early was the difference between the good SEALs and great ones. Discipline is paramount to any leader and any team. When you have the discipline to get up early, you are rewarded with more free time. You can get more done in a given day.

The more discipline you and your team employ, the more freedom you will have to practice "decentralized command". It may seem that having more disciplined procedures would take away freedom; but in fact, "discipline is that pathway to freedom".

Another key to becoming a disciplined leader is knowing your team. It is getting to know them more deeply than you normally would. Ian Mann[2] suggests the concept of hot buttons which he says refers to each person having a different area that is important to them at various stages of their lives.

Getting to know your team means identifying their hot buttons and knowing their motivations, their lives, their families and their interests. A disciplined leader should however never grow so close to a team member that objectivity is lost.

Willink and Babin summarise "the dichotomy of leadership" into clear statements that describe how discipline creates great leaders. A great leader must be:

- Confident but not cocky
- Courageous but not foolhardy
- Competitive, but a gracious loser
- Attentive to details, but not obsessed by them
- Strong but have endurance
- A leader and a follower
- Humble, not passive
- Aggressive, not overbearing
- Quiet, not silent
- Calm, but not robotic
- Logical, but not devoid of emotions

- Close with the troops, but not so close that one becomes more important than another or than the good of the team
- Able to execute extreme ownership while exercising decentralized command
- A good leader has nothing to prove but everything to prove

Being a disciplined leader means that you are prepared to stand your ground at decision time but that you are flexible enough to also accept the input from your team. Remember that you can listen to others' opinion without needing to act upon them because ultimately you are the one that remains accountable.

Leaders that display a strong sense of self-discipline are leaders that know how to control their actions and emotions, and are also leaders that can be trusted to do the right thing.

Use the Discipline Checklist to measure your discipline and self-discipline as a catalyst leader and how you measure. Remember to be honest with yourself because you are the only one who sees this and you alone know if you are being honest.

The score you allocate is based on the scale below where

1. Definitely do not agree
2. Disagree
3. Not sure
4. Agree
5. Definitely agree

SKILL, ATTRIBUTE, ACTION	1	2	3	4	5
You show self-discipline by ensuring that whatever task is at hand gets completed					
You are willing to do things that others do not want to do to get the job done					
You focus on the end result and achieving the objective					
You are flexible enough to get to know your team and what makes them tick					
You accept responsibility for your actions					
TOTAL SCORE OUT OF 25					

EMOTIONALLY INTELLIGENT

Being able to keep your emotions under control when things go wrong is a very important attribute of a leader. As the leader, you are looked to for guidance and support and if you lose control over your emotions in a crisis then you will lose your effectiveness as a leader.

There have been many books written on Emotional Intelligence and we do not want to publish another book on the subject. We do however want to use the concept of emotion and the control of emotions to illustrate how it impacts the success of a leader and your ability to be a catalyst

Emotional intelligence is an awareness of your actions and feelings and how they affect those around you. It also means that you value others, listen to their wants and needs, and is able to empathise or identify with them on many different levels. Emotional intelligence requires the ability to recognise your emotions, understand what these emotions are telling you, and to realise how your emotions affect the people around you. For this reason, emotional intelligence also involves your perception of others: when you understand how they feel it allows you to manage relationships more effectively. We all have different personalities, different wants and needs, and different ways of showing our emotions. If we hope to succeed in life and business, especially as a successful leader, emotional intelligence becomes important.

Leaders with high emotional intelligence are usually successful in the things they do because they are the ones that others want on their team. When people with high emotional intelligence send an email, it gets answered.

When they need help, they get it. Because they make others feel good, they go through life much more easily than people who are easily angered or upset.

Characteristics of Emotional Intelligence

In 1995, Daniel Goleman[3] an American psychologist, developed a framework of five elements that define emotional intelligence:

Self-Awareness

People with high emotional intelligence are usually very self-aware. They understand their emotions, and because of this, they don't let their feelings rule them. They're confident – because they trust their intuition and don't let their emotions get out of control.

They're also willing to take an honest look at themselves. They know their strengths and weaknesses, and they work on these areas so they can perform better. For these reasons self-awareness is arguably the most important part of emotional intelligence.

Self-Regulation

This is the ability to control emotion and impulses. People who self-regulate typically don't allow themselves to become emotionally volatile, and they don't make impulsive, careless decisions. They think before they act. Characteristics of self-regulation are thoughtfulness, comfort with change, integrity and the ability to say - No.

Motivation

People with a high degree of emotional intelligence are usually motivated. They're willing to defer immediate results for long-term success. They're highly productive, love a challenge, and are very effective in whatever they do.

Empathy

This is perhaps the second-most important element of emotional intelligence. Empathy is the ability to identify with and understand the wants, needs, and viewpoints of those around you. People with empathy are good at recognizing the feelings of others, even when those feelings may not be obvious. As a result, empathetic people are usually excellent at managing relationships and listening and relating to others. They avoid stereotyping and judging too quickly, and they live their lives in a very open, honest way.

Social Skills

It's usually much easier to engage with someone who has good social skills, another sign of high emotional intelligence. Those with strong social skills are typically team players. Rather than focus on their own success first, they help others develop and shine. They can manage disputes, are excellent communicators, and are masters at building and maintaining relationships.

As you've probably determined, emotional intelligence can be a key to success in your life – especially in your career. The ability to manage people and relationships is very important in all leaders, so developing and using your emotional intelligence can be a good way to show others the leader inside of you.

How to Improve Your Emotional Intelligence

Emotional intelligence can be learned and developed by applying the following strategies:

Observe how you react to other people, peers and subordinates. Do you rush to judgement before you know all of the facts? Do you resort to stereotyping people? Look honestly at how you think and interact with other people. Try to show empathy and put yourself in their place, and be more open and accepting of their perspectives and needs.

Look at your work environment. Are you continuously looking for praise and attention for your achievements? Remember that humility is a noble quality to possess, and being humble does in no way mean that you're shy or that you lack self-confidence. By being humble, you show everyone that you know what you did, and you can be quietly confident about it. Give others a chance to shine by putting the focus on them, and don't be so caught up with only getting praise for yourself.

Do a self-evaluation. What are your weaknesses? Are you

willing to accept these weaknesses and admit to the fact that you're not that perfect? Are you willing to work on some areas to make yourself a better person? You must have the courage to look at yourself honestly as this is the only way to implement changes in your life.

Examine how you react to stressful situations. Are you overly impatient and do you become upset every time there's a delay or something doesn't happen exactly the way you want it to happen? Do you blame others or become angry at them when things don't go according to plan, even when it's not their fault? The ability to stay calm and in control in difficult situations is a highly-valued attribute both in the business world and outside it. Being emotionally intelligent requires that you learn to keep your emotions in check when things go wrong and chaos ensues.

Take responsibility for your actions. If you hurt someone's feelings, apologise to them directly. Don't ignore what you did or try to avoid the person. If you are honest with yourself and others, and you are upfront about it and show responsibility for your actions, people are usually more willing to forgive and forget, especially if you make an honest attempt to make things right.

Examine how your actions will affect others before you take those actions. The old adage of "look before you leap" definitely applies here. If the decisions you make will impact others, you should put yourself in their place to see what their possible reaction to your decision could be. Ask yourself how will they feel if you do this? Would you want that experience? If you must take action, how can you help others deal with the effects? How do you respond others?

Are you considerate of other people's feelings? What tone do you use when you communicate with your followers?

Remember, affirmation lets the team members know that what they do is important and makes them feel valued.

Use the following Emotional Intelligence Checklist to measure your emotional intelligence as a catalyst leader and how you measure. Remember to be honest with yourself because you are the only one who sees this and you alone know if you are being honest.

The score you allocate is based on the scale below where
1. Definitely do not agree
2. Disagree
3. Not sure
4. Agree

SKILL, ATTRIBUTE, ACTION	1	2	3	4	5
You can keep calm in the midst of a crisis					
You are aware of how your actions and emotions affect others around you					
You can control your emotions effectively					
You are self-motivated and productive					
You can identify with other peoples' needs and wants					
Total Score out of 25					

NOTES

REASONABLE

To be reasonable means to be of sound judgement, but also to be fair and practical. It means that you allow creativity in your team and you are also lenient when they make mistakes. Being reasonable also means that you are fair in all your dealings with the team and that you do not embarrass them publicly.

As a reasonable leader, you further have to examine your values and beliefs. Are these values (your vision or message) sound beliefs and how strictly do you enforce them? Are you convinced that your values and beliefs as the leader are the correct ones? Are you prepared to accept new ideas?

As a reasonable leader, you would be firm in your convictions of your values and message while at the same time still being open to new ideas. What we mean by this is that even though you are convinced of your message (values and beliefs) and you determinately drive that message to your followers and do not allow anyone to sway you from your message, where there are better ways of implementing your message, you are still prepared to listen to them. This is the difference between a reasonable leader and an autocratic leader.

Hitler had a message, to develop an Aryan race that was superior to other races. Pure blood Germans that could control the world. He was convinced of his beliefs and values and adamantly drove the message. Hitler however, was a dictator and an autocratic leader as he eliminated anyone who opposed him or his message. A reasonable leader would have been open to suggestions and even though they would not necessarily have accepted or implemented these suggestions, they nevertheless would have listened and considered them.

Reasonable leaders lead with an implied authority. They are able to convince their team to carry out the actions required in order to achieve the end result. They do not have to be instructed or forced to act, instead they do it because they actually want to.

A leader must have the ability to be pragmatic and deal with the reality of the situation, applying it to their leadership in a way is what makes them reasonable. No leader, no matter how informed, is always right. It is pertinent to be as informed as possible, allowing yourself to have a better understanding the circumstances in which you operate.

The difference between reality and perception is quite distinct and quite crucial to leadership. The true reality is one that considers other factors and people involved, and is the basis for informed decision making. To make informed decisions, a leader must be willing to acknowledge and heed the perceptions and perspectives of others to consider all possible outcomes. In studying all factors in a scenario from all possible perspectives, a leader can then arrive at a reality.

Being reasonable as a leader is the best way to maximize your positive leadership traits. Reasonable leaders are the leaders that team members and followers find admirable, approachable, and inspiring. Contrary to popular belief, you can be reasonable without compromising your ability to be daring, bold, innovative, or imaginative. You can have all of those characteristics and if you are prepared as a leader to consider a variety of viewpoints and collect and analyse all of the information you need to make decisions, you can be a positive, reasonable leader.

Being humane, according to the dictionary means showing understanding (empathy) and having a rapport with others. It means that you have the ability to be empathetic and place yourself in the other person's shoes.

Creating a business and implementing your vision or message often involves a bit of forecasting. Especially so in the beginning stages of the business, where you need to be constantly inspiring your team to see the vision of the end goal and the subsequent successes to come through implementation, is vital. Keep your team informed through regular communication and feedback to make your team feel they have invested in the achievements of the company. Whether you use a reward or recognition system, generating enthusiasm for the hard work they are all putting in is very important.

Being able to inspire your team is great for focusing on the future goals, but it is also important for the current issues. When you are engrossed in your work so deeply and morale is low, or energy levels are sapped, recognise that we all need a break from time to time. It is your job to keep spirits up, and that begins with an appreciation for the hard work. Give recognition where it is due for the work that has been achieved and commend the team on each of their efforts.

A basic concept of leadership that is so often overlooked is that not all human beings are the same. We all have cultural perspectives, language barriers, different educational backgrounds, personality traits and varying value systems with which individuals come pre-conditioned that greatly affects how information is processed and interpreted. Some people work well under pressure, others don't.

Some respond well to tough love, while others will take it personally and put up a wall. To ensure your effectiveness as a leader, you must possess the ability to vary your leadership approach based on the person and on the situation at hand. Your ability to execute this principle will play a huge role in your ability to get your team to give their best and become your partners along the journey to fulfilling the vision or message.

Another aspect of being reasonable is to allow your followers to make mistakes. This concept will be explored further in Part 2. As long as they learn from the failures, they should be allowed to try and fail from time to time.

Whether you employ an open-door policy, or you make a point of talking to your followers on a regular basis, making yourself available to discuss on-the-job issues is important. Your team will learn to trust and depend on you, and will be not be hesitant to work harder.

Use the following Reasonable Checklist to measure how reasonable you are as a catalyst leader and how you measure. Remember to be honest with yourself because you are the only one who sees this and you alone know if you are being honest.

The score you allocate is based on the scale below where

     1.   Definitely do not agree
     2.   Disagree
     3.   Not sure
     4.   Agree
     5.   Definitely agree

SKILL, ATTRIBUTE, ACTION	1	2	3	4	5
You are willing to consider the input and ideas of others					
You can show empathy by putting yourself in someone else's' shoes					
You are prepared to inspire and reward others					
You are considerate of others' backgrounds and culture					
You have an open-door practice					
TOTAL SCORE OUT OF 25					

NOTES

SINCERE

Sincerity and integrity lays the foundation for trust and respect and requires that the actions of the leader reflects the values of the organisation.

Not all the decisions you make will be so clear-cut or open for discussion. You may be forced at times to deviate from your set course and make off-the-cuff decisions. This is where your reliability and consistency in decision making will prove to be vital. It is during these critical moments that your team will look to you for guidance and you may be forced to make a quick decision. As a leader, it's important to remember to keep the ultimate goal in sight and be consistent in the way you make these decisions. Your team needs to learn to depend on your decision-making skills and to trust you to make the best possible decisions that will benefit the organisation. By being reliable and consistent you will show your team that they can trust the decisions you make and therefore also put in the necessary effort to achieve the end goal.

When leading a team through uncharted waters, there is no roadmap on what to do. Everything is uncertain, and the higher the risk, the higher the pressure. That is where your reliability will be tested. Guiding your team through the process of your day-to-day tasks can be honed down to a science. But when something unexpected occurs, or you are thrown into a new scenario, your team will look to you for guidance. If you have proved you are reliable in these situations, your team will learn to trust you. Learning to trust yourself is as important as your team learning to trust you.

Moral Compass

Without clear fundamental principles people simply accept the norms and values through repetition and because it just happens to exist.

It is necessary for people to define and what they believe and value in order that people can act on them. The same principle applies to ethics. Creating a clear list of core ethical principles as a Moral Compass[4] would provide a benchmark against which ethics could be measured.

If you write down a list of moral values and expect that list to be taken seriously, the moral values has to be consistent with each other, cover all the gaps and be morally acceptable. If this were not the case your list would have very little credibility.

Consistent means that the values or beliefs agree with each other. You cannot declare "I will accept men and women as equals," and then also declare that "All women should obey men and be subservient to them". The longer a list of moral values is, the more difficult it is to make it consistent, whilst a shorter list has to stick to more basic and fundamental statements.

There must not be any gaps in your list. People must not be in a position to start questioning parts of your list. If you say you will not lie then people may ask, but what if you did not lie but just left out certain truths.

Morality isn't defined by what it is, but by what it does. Moral values are how you measure the difference between right and wrong, between good and bad, between positive and negative action.

The four points of the Moral Compass are discussed in more detail below.

Integrity

- Telling the truth
- Standing up for what is right
- Keeping promises
- Acting consistently with universal principles, personal values and beliefs

Integrity is the concept of basing of one's actions on an internally consistent framework of principles. You are said to have integrity to the extent that everything you do is based on the same core set of values. While those values may change, there is always a consistency between your values and your actions.

Integrity can be expressed as personal honesty: acting according to your beliefs and values at all times. Integrity can be seen as doing the right thing even when no one is watching.

Integrity requires that accountability and moral responsibility are necessary for maintaining consistency between your actions and your principles.

Measuring Integrity

In most cases, there is no middle ground when it comes to measuring integrity. You either have integrity or not. People talk about someone having integrity or someone lacking integrity, which then implies they have NO integrity.

Integrity has strong links to honesty and in business it usually boils down to companies trying to identify the facts that are left out of the discussion that could place a negative effect on the perception of the person.

Honesty

Honesty is the human quality of communicating and acting truthfully where truth is seen as a value. This includes listening as well as speaking.

Superficially, honesty means simply stating facts and views as best you truly believe them to be. It includes both honesty to others, and to you and about your own motives and inner beliefs. Honesty sometimes has a negative effect (unpopularity) for someone has the ability to cause misfortune to the person who displays it. The concept of honesty applies to all behaviours.

Responsibility

- Taking responsibility for personal choices
- Admitting one's mistakes and failures
- Embracing responsibility for serving others

Corporate Social Responsibility

This is where organisations consider the interests of society by taking responsibility for the impact of their activities on customers, suppliers, employees, shareholders, communities and other stakeholders, as well as the environment. This obligation is seen to extend beyond the statutory obligation to comply with legislation and sees organisations voluntarily taking further steps to improve the quality of life for employees and their families as well as for the local community and society at large.

Some people may argue that corporations benefit in multiple ways by operating with a perspective broader and longer than their own immediate, short-term profits, while others still argue that it is nothing more than superficial window-dressing.

Moral Responsibility

This can refer to two different but related things.

First, a person has moral responsibility for a situation if that person has an obligation to ensure that something happens. Assume that John promises to baby-sit for his neighbour while she goes to a job interview. However, he decides he will go to a concert instead. Arguably, John has moral responsibility for finding another appropriate babysitter for his neighbour.

- An example of this would be that you learn, understand and adhere to the working hours of your business. You are not being responsible if you are arriving late or leaving work early on a regular basis.

- You create a bad impression with your fellow workers (colleagues) and also with your customers

- You also have a responsibility towards the management who employed you to adhere to the hours of work that were agreed upon when you were employed

Second, a person has moral responsibility for a situation when it would be correct to morally praise or blame that person for the situation. If John fails to find an appropriate babysitter, then he might be said to have moral responsibility for his neighbour's failure to make her job interview.

- If you stay off work or arrive late and leave early all the time, you could be responsible for your store not achieving its targets.

Other areas where it is important to act responsibly and keep your colleagues and management up to date with your movements is:

When you know you will be absent from work;
- The law states that an employee should notify the work before 10am on the day they will be off sick

When you are going on leave
- If you just go off on leave you might have left customer orders unfinished, projects incomplete or jobs half done.

If you are leaving your work station for any reason
- By not informing the other staff, you could have people   searching for you for a variety of reasons and it may be   urgent, but because you notified no-one, it will cause a lot of confusion

Compassion

- Actively caring for others

Compassion is a human emotion prompted by the pain of others. Compassion is more vigorous than empathy and the feeling commonly gives rise to an active desire to alleviate another's suffering. In ethical terms, the Golden Rule passed down through the ages is: Do to others as you would have done to you. Compassion is considered in all the major religious traditions as among the greatest of virtues.

One of the ways that compassion can be demonstrated is by adhering to the various policies and procedures in the organisation. These could include any of the following policies (including legislation applicable):

- Smoking in the workplace
- Eating and drinking on the shop floor
- Dress code and grooming habits

Forgiveness

- Letting go of your own mistakes
- Letting go of others' mistakes

Forgiveness is the process of ceasing to feel resentment, indignation or anger for a perceived offense, difference or mistake, or ceasing to demand punishment or restitution.

This definition, however, is subject to much philosophical critique.

Forgiveness may be considered simply in terms of the person who forgives, in terms of the person forgiven and/

or in terms of the relationship between the forgiver and the person forgiven. In some contexts, it may be granted without any expectation of compensation, and without any response on the part of the offender (for example, one may forgive a person who is dead). In practical terms, it may be necessary for the offender to offer some form of acknowledgment, apology, and/or restitution, or even just ask for forgiveness, in order for the wronged person to believe they are able to forgive.

Most world religions include teachings on the nature of forgiveness, and many of these teachings provide an underlying basis for many varying modern-day traditions and practices of forgiveness. However, throughout the ages, philosophers have studied forgiveness apart from religion. The need to forgive is widely recognised by the public, but they are often at a loss for ways to accomplish it.

Studies show that people who forgive are happier and healthier than those who hold resentments. One study has shown that the positive benefit of forgiveness is similar whether it was based upon religious or secular counselling as opposed to a control group that received no forgiveness counselling.

Use the following Sincere Checklist to measure your sincerity as a catalyst leader and how you measure. Remember to be honest with yourself because you are the only one who sees this and you alone know if you are being honest.

The score you allocate is based on the scale below where
1. Definitely do not agree
2. Disagree
3. Not sure
4. Agree
5. Definitely agree

SKILL, ATTRIBUTE, ACTION	1	2	3	4	5
You display a level of integrity in your decision making that allows people to fully trust you and your actions					
You have a non-negotiable set of core values and you stand on these values					
You are always honest even it makes you unpopular					
You are compassionate and you consider the feelings of others					
You are prepared to forgive peoples mistakes and failures especially where a lesson has been learned					
TOTAL SCORE OUT OF 25					

NOTES

53

HUMBLE

Leaders that truly are catalysts need to be humble. Being humble does not mean that you cave into any adversity or that you do not exert your authority as required. No, being humble implies that as a leader you are often times prepared to take the back seat and let the team members who have more proficient skills in a particular area apply their skills to complete the task or solve the problem.

Being humble means that you as the leader accept that you are not necessarily the expert in every situation and that the reason you have a team of followers is that they too possess certain skills. If you harness those skills you can better achieve your end goal or objective

Humility also can include servant leadership.

The assumption is that if leaders focus on the needs and desires of followers, followers will reciprocate through increased teamwork, deeper engagement, and better performance.

Robert Greenleaf[5] identified 10 characteristics of a Servant Leader. These characteristics, described below, show how a servant leader can also display humility and be an effective leader and catalyst. The 10 characteristics are as follows:

1. **Listening**.

     Through being humble, the leader seeks to identify the will of a group and helps clarify that will. He or she seeks to listen receptively to what is being said.

2. **Empathy**   .

     The servant-leader strives to understand and empathize with others as has been described in detail in the attribute of Reasonable.

3. **Healing**   .

     Many people have suffered from a variety of emotional hurts and the humble leaders recognize that they also have an opportunity to help heal those they come into contact with.

4. **Awareness** .

     General awareness, and especially self-awareness, strengthens the humble leader.

5. **Persuasion** .

     The humble-leader seeks to convince others rather than enforce compliance.

6. **Conceptualization**.

     Humble leaders seek to nurture their abilities to look at a problem from a conceptualizing perspective that means that one must think beyond day-to-day realities.

7. **Foresight**

    Foresight enables the humble leader to understand the lessons from the past, the realities of the present, and the likely consequence of a decision for the future.

8. **Stewardship**.

    Stewardship in a humble leader emphasizes the use of openness and persuasion rather than control.

9. **Commitment to the growth of people**.

    A humble leader is deeply committed to the growth of each and every individual within the institution.

10. **Building community**.

    A humble leader seeks to identify some means for building community among those who work within a given institution.

"I believe we are all equal in this world — Unfortunately, status and money often affect others' perceptions. Not only do I respond to everybody I possibly can because of my belief, but also: I will never forget what it felt like to be ignored by 'influencers' when I first started out. This ignorance doesn't make sense to me because an audience makes an influencer. The rewarding responses from many people make it all worthwhile - I have received some truly memorable words of respect and love! We all start somewhere. Given the chance; we can all get somewhere, too." Sam Hurley

Use the following Humble Checklist to measure your humility as a catalyst leader and how you measure. The score you allocate, is based on the scale below where

1. Definitely do not agree
2. Disagree
3. Not sure
4. Agree
5. Definitely agree

SKILL, ATTRIBUTE, ACTION	1	2	3	4	5
You are prepared to sometimes take the back seat and let someone else have the limelight					
You realise that you are not always the expert and let others dominate the situation					
You are a good listener and get all the facts before you act					
Your approach to leadership is to entice rather than control					
You are aware that some people need to deal with emotional issues and you allow them time to "heal"					
TOTAL SCORE OUT OF 25					

NOTES

INFORMATION

The sharing of information is vital in any business today. If your janitor does not know where the company is going, or what their vision or mission is, how do you expect him to put in the required work effort to assist the company with achieving their vision? The vision, or message of the company, is not for the exclusive right of top management or the executive only, it is to be communicated to, and understood by, every single employee in the organisation.

The janitor, even though he has tasks that might not appear that important, was appointed to the position of janitor because his function was an integral part in achieving the overall objective.

By not communicating the vision, mission and core values to the janitor, you could in fact jeopardise the entire success of the organisation. The janitor also needs to be part of the culture of the organisation, and this culture is created through the core values.

So, you can see that ensuring the flow of information to each individual in the organisation, no matter how unimportant you may consider their job or contribution to be, is a vital part of the success of the organisation and you as the leader. Knowing what you want accomplished may seem clear in your head, but if you try to explain it to someone else and are met with a blank expression, you know there is a problem with the picture that now appears inside their head. If this has happened to you then you may want to focus on honing your communication skills.

Clarity is all about having the ability to explain in sufficient detail exactly what you are expecting in a way that the other person understands exactly what you want.

Being able to clearly and succinctly describe what you want done in a sensitive way is extremely important. If you can't relate your vision to your team, you won't all be working towards the same goal.

Training new members and creating a productive work environment all depend on healthy lines of communication.

Another vital aspect of sharing information is the impact it has on raising morale and motivational levels. Empowering your team members is also a means of sharing information.

A leader, according to John C. Maxwell[6], goes through various developmental stages to become a successful leader. According to Maxwell, a leader only achieves Level 5 when they have the ability to develop other leaders, not followers. Maxwell also claims that only leaders can train leaders. If you have no knowledge or experience as a leader, it is impossible to train or develop other leaders.

Empowering your followers is just as important as developing future leaders empowering your people to work, learn and grow together as a team and to harvest the full potential of the team.

Streamlining the vision is essential towards creating an organised and efficient business, but if you don't learn to trust your team with that vision, you might never progress to the next stage. It's important to remember that trusting your team with your idea is a sign of strength, and not a sign of weakness.

Delegating tasks to the appropriate people or departments is one of the most important skills you can develop as your business grows. The emails and tasks will begin to pile up, and the more you stretch yourself thin, the lower the quality of your work will become, and the less you will produce.

The key to delegation is identifying the strengths of your team, and capitalising on them. Find out what each team member enjoys doing most and assign task accordingly. Chances are they'll find that task more enjoyable, they will likely put more thought and effort behind it. This will not only prove to your team that you trust and believe in them, but will also free up your time to focus on the higher-level tasks, that should not be delegated. It's a fine balance, but one that will have a great impact on the productivity of your business.

Effective delegation develops people who are ultimately more fulfilled and productive. Leaders become more fulfilled and productive themselves as they learn to count on their staff and are freed up to attend to more strategic issues.

Delegation is often very difficult for new team leaders and managers who feel the need to remain in control. Making the same decisions they have always made makes them feel comfortable. They believe they can do a better job themselves. They don't want to risk losing any of their power and stature and quite often, they don't want to risk giving authority to subordinates in case they fail and impair the organisation.

Delegation is one of the most important leadership skills. These logical rules and techniques will help you to delegate well (and will help you to help your manager when you are being delegated a task or new responsibility - delegation is a two-way process).

Good delegation:
- saves you time,
- develops your people,
- grooms a successor,
- and motivates.

Poor delegation will:
- cause you frustration,
- demotivate and confuse the other person,
- and fail to achieve the task or purpose itself.

Becoming good at effective delegation is a leadership skill that's worth improving. Here are the simple steps to follow if you want to get delegation right, with different levels of delegation freedom that you can offer.

Delegation is a very helpful aid for succession planning, personal development - and seeking and encouraging promotion. It's how we grow in the job - delegation enables us to gain experience to take on higher responsibilities.

Effective delegation is actually crucial for effective succession. For the successor and for the leader too: the main task of a leader in a growing thriving organisation is ultimately to develop a successor. When this happens, everyone can move on to higher things. When it fails to happen the succession and progression becomes dependent on bringing in new people from outside.

Many of us battle daily with **Important** vs **Urgent**. In the current work environment, you are often faced with the problem of having to work overtime a lot due to constantly being in crisis mode where you have to sort out matters that have become **urgent**. All the **urgent** matters were once **important**.

Important matters can be identified as anything that fits with your company's vision and mission. If what you're busy with does not help grow your company's mission and doesn't fit the carefully structured path towards the vision then it is **NOT important**. Even when the matter has moved and feels as if it needs immediate attention, if it doesn't fit with the mission and vision then it isn't **important** and so you should leave it out.

When does an **important** matter become **urgent**? The simplest answer is poor planning either on your part or due to poor planning by someone else.

We tend to very easily confuse **important** with **urgent** and then refer to all our **important** work as **urgent**. In short, **important** refers to a task that directly impacts your vision or message, whereas **urgent** means you have run out of the time needed to complete what was **important**.

We consulted a client of ours last year where the finance department staff were involved more in logistics functions than financial functions. They spent most of their time and efforts arranging deliveries and collections. If their vision was to give accurate information to the board, it would have been more efficient if the company employed a logistics person instead.

That said, the poor clerks in the Finance department were on the phone during the day sorting out logistical issues, but then over weekends they had to work overtime to catch up on the financial tasks.

We calculated the time they spent on the phone solving operational and logistical issues and found that, because there was no vision in place for the department, they reverted back to the vision of the company, thus helping all the other departments achieve their goals and spent eight hours a week on the phone with non-finance activities and had to work on Saturdays to make up for the mismanaged time.

They were constantly busy with another department's *important* work that due to poor resources management had now become *urgent* and in the process the work of the finance department had now moved to being *urgent* because of the loss of time.

Due to poor planning and lack of proper information sharing, the finance department had to incur additional costs and sacrifice their weekends and family time to catch up on the lost work that was the function of their department.

The impact then was:

- There was a direct impact as the staff were overworked and demoralized because of the long hours and not having enough time to rest and spend with their loved ones.

- There was a financial impact on the bottom line of the company due to the increased salary costs because unnecessary overtime was being paid.

This whole problem could have been solved if there was a singular message for that specific department communicated with conviction that was clearly understood by all employees in the department.

Ensure that the message is aligned to the company's vision or message but still remains applicable to the department. Constantly communicate that message with clarity and conviction. This will prevent employees being confused about their role in delivering on the message and not get involved in activities that do not align to the message of that department.

Therefore, as a catalyst leader you must communicate the message clearly and not allow any activities in your department or company that do not align to the message.

Use the following Information Checklist to measure your ability as a catalyst leader and how you measure. Remember to be honest with yourself because you are the only one who sees this and you alone know if you are being honest.

The score you allocate, is based on the scale below where

1.   Definitely do not agree
2.   Disagree
3.   Not sure
4.   Agree
5.   Definitely agree

SKILL, ATTRIBUTE, ACTION	1	2	3	4	5
My division or department has a clear message or vision					
The message for my division or department is clearly communicated to me on a regular basis					
My division or department only conducts activities that align directly to the message or vision for my department or division					
Information is shared that is relevant to the departmental message					
The message for my department is clearly understood by all					
Total Score out of 25					

NOTES

67

PASSION

Passion is a word that we constantly use without fully understanding the different connotations and denotations attached to it.

- Passion is not love, yet the same strong fondness or emotions are present when you are "in love".
- How do you identify someone with passion?
- How can you nurture your passion for your staff as a leader?

Passion is that sense of devotion and dedication that drives you. It is what makes you get out of bed every morning with intensity. Passion is what propels you into action. Passion is not vision or mission, passion is what drives you to achieve you vision and mission. Vision is the long-term goal. Mission is what actions one takes to translate that vision into reality. Vision is what you want to do with your existence, and mission is how you will go about it. Simply put; passion is what makes you exist

What corporations, organisations, and governments should invest in is a passion statement and not necessarily a vision statement. Your passion statement should be a declaration of why you exist as an entity and what drives you.

There is a difference between management and leadership. Though many think the two are interchangeable. They are not. Leadership is action, not just a position. Not all leaders are managers and vice versa. But there are rare individuals who are both.

Passion has the capacity to translate vision into reality. Without passion, leaders are just mere visionaries. Passion is the distinction between success and failure. True passion is that fire that never stops burning. Becomes the catalyst!

In 2017 we visited a company to evaluate their current operating and company procedures. We also evaluated how they could implement ways and measures to increase their turnover. Furthermore, we investigated methods which would allow them to implement a better marketing strategy and raise their overall level of customer service.

The owner had given up the fight and spent the entire time we were there justifying why he felt so strongly about not being able to make the company work and we would not be able to implement any actions that would take the company out of the current slump that it was in.

According to him they were already fighting hard against all the elements that had caused the business to be in decline. He was well prepared to engage in a debate focusing on all the reasons for failure; he blamed the economy for not having fully recovered from the global slump in 2008; he blamed the high staff turnover and their lack of commitment; he blamed the Human Resources department for not employing the correct staff who were properly trained and motivated; he blamed the lack of local support from the community and his target market; he blamed the lack of stake holder interest and he felt overworked. At one stage, he even felt that he was working with incompetent people.

He was so emotionally deflated that we really did not know what to say to him to get him out of this sad state. He was on the verge of packing up and giving everything away.

At this point we asked him a simple straightforward question: Why did you start this business? Without a moment's hesitation, he proceeded to take us on a historical journey of how he had passionately started the business, how he had really wanted to help people achieve their dreams and how he had the solution to make the world a better place.

Suddenly he had his passion back, he looked back and reminded himself why he started this business in the first place, and that this passion was bigger than the problems he currently faced. The trigger was his own passion, which somehow over the years had become deeply buried under a huge pile of excuses.

His reignited passion became his motivator. The flicker in his eyes was back, and in matter of twenty minutes he had found his driving force and had his fire back.

There is a story in the Bible, in Matthew 14 where the disciple Peter gets out the boat and walks on the water. His goal was to walk towards Jesus, the moment he took his eyes of the goal, and started to focus on how big the waves were, he started to sink.

Whether you are a believer in the Bible or not is not the point, the point of the illustration is that as soon as you take your eyes off the goal you are aiming for, you will sink. You will be in the same state as the owner who took his eyes off his passion and lost that vital spark to keep going.

Henry Ford said it brilliantly; "An obstacle is that frightful thing you see when you take your eyes of the goal." These obstacles in life drain our passion.

Passion is driven by the belief of what is not known as a fact yet. That belief that you will arrive at the end destination even though the rocky road you are traveling at the moment may be strewn with obstacles.

As an entrepreneur, leader or just a common blue-collar worker, you have two choices. Say what the people want to hear, do what they want you to do, and find all the right excuses why you don't succeed; or start to sincerely and passionately care about what you do and say. Care about how you present yourself in the workplace. Become passionate again about the reason why you started out on this journey in the first place.

Become passionate again about why you are right here, right now. Ask yourself: "Would you believe in a person that does not believe in himself?"

Use the following Passion Checklist to measure your passion as a catalyst leader and how you measure. Remember to be honest with yourself because you are the only one who sees this and you alone know if you are being honest.

The score you allocate, is based on the scale below where

1.   Definitely do not agree
2.   Disagree
3.   Not sure
4.   Agree
5.   Definitely agree

SKILL, ATTRIBUTE, ACTION	1	2	3	4	5
You are a go-getter and self motivated and excited about what you believe					
You drive your message with conviction and determination showing complete enthusiasm					
You have complete faith in your future and you know where you are headed					
You passion for your message is so strong that you can influence others to believe your message					
You follow through on your message and vision and do not give up on your message					
TOTAL SCORE OUT OF 25					

NOTES

THE TEST

Let us look at a practical example of how a leader applies the Leadership Flag incorporating the message and catalyst concept.

Jesus was the one of the most effective leaders ever in that He not only managed to create a following of over 2,4 billion people worldwide, which represents more than one third (33%) of the entire global population, but this following grew after He was no longer on earth.

He had one message: "I have good news, God Loves you." He became a mentor to twelve disciples (followers) and even though one of them betrayed him it did not distract Him from His message nor did it make Him less of a leader. In fact, we could probably argue, based on the size of His followers alone, that He was the greatest leader of all.

Jesus' message was so powerful and the belief in Him and His message by His eleven (there were many more later) remaining mentees (disciples), that they took that message and became leaders themselves. They started what today is known as Christianity, a religion which was very small during their period. These twelve men, and those that followed, became catalysts for others to also became leaders such as Paul.

Do you want to become a catalyst? What impact would you make if 2.4 billion people followed your message?

As we mentioned previously, Jesus also possessed the attributes of the Leadership Flag as shown here.

Lifestyle

The Bible tells us He had no sin. His entire lifestyle was to promote the Kingdom of God and He lived that lifestyle to the end.

Example

He was an example in every way. He never committed any wrongdoing according to the Jewish laws of the time. At the end, when He was crucified, the only charge they could come up with was being the King of the Jews.

Authority

According to the disciples Matthew, Mark, Luke and John's records and accounts of the time, when Jesus spoke people listened. He preached to crowds of more than 3000 and 5000 (according to the records those figures did not even include the women and children that were present).

Discipline

Every night He went up the Mount of Olives to pray to God for four hours. He understood the importance of having His own Mentor.

He was disciplined enough to make it part of His routine.

Emotionally Intelligent

In John 11:34 – when Lazarus died, we are told that Jesus wept. This showed that Jesus had emotions. There was a time when he got angry and overturned the tables of the money-changers in the synagogue but Jesus showed that He was emotionally intelligent by not over-reacting to situations. He was tempted to react many times when the Pharisees and Sadducees tried to trick Him with wily questions.

Reasonable

Jesus was always reasonable because He treated everyone fairly and allowed them to make failures. Even when Judas betrayed Him, Jesus did not condemn him. Jesus provided sound advice that helped people improve their lives.

Sincere

When the Scribes and Pharisees tried to trick Jesus in condemning the woman who was accused of adultery, He bowed down and wrote something in the sand, maybe the sins of the accusers, who knows, but what He did next, no one expected. You must understand that adultery in the time of Jesus was punishable by being stoned to death, yet He did not condemn her, He asked her accusers to pick up the first stone if they were without sin. Being consistent in His message He also instructed the woman to not sin anymore showing that sincerity does not mean letting it slide.

Humble

In John chapter 4, Jesus was speaking to a Samaritan woman. When His disciples returned, and asked Him why He was speaking to her as the custom in those days was that the Jews and Samaritans did not mingle and chat to each other. Jesus' leadership style was such that He was all inclusive and even though He was Jew and considered to be part of a chosen race, His humble behaviour was the catalyst for anti-racism. Jesus did not discriminate against anyone, not even children or diseased people.

Information

He was a wealth of information. He was very young when he was found with the priests and scriptural intellectuals in the temple, discussing God's Word. He was a specialist in the field. Jesus also ensured that His followers and the crowds in general understood His message that is why He always explained His message in parables or stories.

Passion

He was passionate about His message. He drove it with everything He had and was even prepared to give His life for the message. Even on the cross, he preached it to the fellow convict that was about to die with him.

SELF-EVALUATION

Use the following table to measure your Leadership Flag skills as a catalyst leader. Use the total score from each of the previous checklists you completed for each of the ten Leadership Flag attributes.

LEADERSHIP FLAG ATTRIBUTE	SCORE
Lifestyle	
Example	
Authority	
Discipline	
Emotionally Intelligent	
Reasonable	
Sincere	
Humble	
Information	
Passion	
TOTAL SCORE OUT OF 250	

To rate yourself as a Catalyst Leader, consider the following:

If your score was between 0 and 100 you have a huge gap in your leadership armoury and you would need to get help to develop the required skills to become a catalyst leader

If you score was between 100 and 200 you are getting by as a leader but you are not instilling the flame or creating the spark required of a leader to be a catalyst. You need to identify your areas of weakness and hone those skills so you can become a catalyst

If your score was 180 and higher you have developed the skills required to get the best out of your followers and keep the flame burning. Live your message with passion and become the catalyst to as many as you can.

NOTES

part 2

THE LEADERSHIP FORMULA

DEMYSTIFYING THE LEADERSHIP FORMULA

Leadership can be considered a science in as far as it is something that can be tested and proven. Therefore it is possible to develop a basic formula to provide the guidelines to becoming a great leader. We believe that great leaders are not necessarily born that way, but that through observation of the behaviours and practices of successful and great leaders, and a successful mentorship programme, you can learn to also be a great leader.

By observing the great leaders of our times and modelling their behaviours into a formula, we can provide the requirements for becoming a great leader. The coaching and training therefore assist in developing these leadership skills and by mentoring the mentee correctly we can enforce these behaviours and skills as depicted in the formula to develop individuals into great leaders.

Great leadership can be broken down into a simple formula. This formula is in no way a mathematical formula but merely a tool to demonstrate the interdependence of the various elements in the concept.

The formula for leadership is expressed as

$$M^s \times nM^e = C^n$$

M^s = Message
M^e = Mentor / Mentee
n = number of mentees or duplication of catalyst
C= Catalyst

Message

Your message is what drives you. It is your vision or those goals you have set for yourself that continuously propel you forward. As a business, you need to have an indication of where you are going and how you plan on getting there and as important as it is for you to know where you are going it is even more so for others to know. If you do not know where you are headed then how do you ever expect to convince anyone to follow you and if they won't follow you then they won't help you reach your goal.

The formula elements for a message is then as follows:

Message = Conviction + Passion + Determination

- **Conviction** = believe your message/vision, live your message, be the message.
  PLUS
- **Passion** = be passionate about your message and communicate the message to your followers in detail.
  PLUS
- **Determination** = Show resilience even in the face of adversity or when no-one believes in your message. Show tenacity and push through.

Conviction

Conviction is the complete belief in your vision or message to the point where you become absolutely passionate about it. You need to spend each waking moment honing your message and living it. If you believe fully in your message it will show and others will follow suit and they will also strive to achieve your message.

Similarly, Millennials depend so heavily on social media, that they appear not to trust anything else other than messages received via social media platforms such as Facebook, Twitter, etc. You should be so convinced of your message that it becomes your passion to the point where you cannot live without it

As a leader your vision, which is your message, how you plan on delivering, implementing and enforcing your message, should be clear. Do not have mixed messages and do not have weak messages that do not inspire and definitely do not have more than one message at a time.

Furthermore, you should have a set of core values. Those non-negotiable values that are the backbone of your message that set you apart from other leaders.

These values need to be the pillars you base your message on and the lifeblood of your team. As mentioned earlier though, you should not be dictatorial about enforcing your message but remain reasonable and open to suggestions while you are rigorously driving your message home.

Passion

Passion is that fire that burns within you for your message. Where passion differs from conviction is, with conviction you believe in your message, but with passion you want to share and spread your message with everyone around you.

If you are passionate about your message you will be talking about it constantly at every opportunity that presents itself. You will be spending all your time, energy and resources getting others, your followers, to buy into this message of yours.

The beauty of being so passionate about your message that you spend as much time as possible trying to get others to buy into it, is that your attitude and actions demonstrate that enthusiasm. People will see your excitement and wonder what it is all about and they will want some of that excitement for themselves.

Passion is the single most important factor for continued success for any company. Once you've lost your passion then you have lost. If you feel like you are losing your passion then refer back to your message and ask yourself why you started down this road in the first place to help guide you back onto it.

Determination

Determination is the tenacity to not give up on your message no matter what the doomsday prophets have to say. You need to have the same tenacity as a bull-terrier that has locked its jaws after biting onto something and that it then takes and immense amount of effort to get him to let go.

There will always be someone who does not see the benefit and success of your message the way you do. People will find all types of excuses to attempt to convince you that the message is wrong – the message won't work – you're too young – you do not have the experience necessary to make the message work. Don't let other people who do not have the same vision and passion you have pull you down or let you lose focus of your message.

Let us look at some examples of famous people throughout history that had to face failure and struggles to achieve something more, the ones that persevered and showed great determination even though others did not believe in them.

Richard Branson, who struggled with dyslexia, had a difficult time with educational institutions. He nearly failed out of the all-boys Scaitcliffe School, which he attended until the age of 13. He then transferred to Stowe School, a boarding school in Stowe, Buckinghamshire, England.

Still struggling, Branson dropped out at the age of 16 to start a youth-culture magazine called **Student**. The publication, run by students, for students, sold $8,000 worth of advertising in its first edition, which was launched in 1966. The first run of 50,000 copies was distributed for free, after Branson covered the costs with advertising

Thomas Edison's teachers said he was "too stupid to learn anything." He was fired from his first two jobs for being "non-productive." As an inventor, Edison made 1,000 unsuccessful attempts at inventing the light bulb. When a reporter asked, "How did it feel to fail 1,000 times?" Edison replied, "I didn't fail 1,000 times. The light bulb was an invention with 1,000 steps

Imagine if **Colonel Harland David Sanders** had not been determined and believed in himself and his product. We would not have enjoyed KFC, the famous chicken made from 11 secrets herbs and spices, world-wide today. Colonel Sanders of Kentucky Fried Chicken fame, Sanders had a hard time selling his chicken at first. In fact, his famous secret chicken recipe was rejected 1,009 times before a restaurant accepted it.

Felix Kjellberg; better known by his online pseudonym of **PewDiePie**; currently holds the largest subscriber count of any YouTube creator. Early in 2017 he caused an uproar across social media platforms and traditional publications such as the Wall Street Journal with a joke that was seen as anti-Semitic. Due to the controversy behind the joke, Kjellberg lost contracts with Disney and YouTube. His premium channel **Scare PewDiePie** was cancelled by YouTube and he lost many sponsors. He faced what seemed a never-ending onslaught of vitriol from other YouTube creators who eagerly pounced to give their view on Kjellberg personally and his content.

It would have been the far easier choice to give up, shut down his channel and admit defeat. However, instead of shutting down his channel, he apologised for the joke and was determined to keep producing videos. He soon found that his loyal follower base was eager to keep supporting him and his subscriber count has since increased to over 50 million subscribers.

These are just some examples of well-known figures throughout history that have shown determination and resilience in the face of challenge and adversity. Imagine where we would be if they had given up on their message or vision.

Some people thrive in the face of setbacks, while others seem unable to recover from them. How would you respond if you lost your job or did not get that promotion that was promised to you? Would regaining your confidence be fairly easy, or very difficult?

There are three basic qualities which you can develop that will help you become the type of person who rebounds from these types of setbacks:

- Try seeing reality clearly. Resilient people have down-to-earth views on the situations they face. They aren't overly optimistic, and they don't deny reality. Instead, they face these harrowing situations, viewing them as a way to train themselves in how to survive hardships.

- See if you can find meaning in what happens. People who bounce back devise constructs about their suffering to create some sort of meaning for themselves and others. You need to learn from the situation.

- Make do with the resources and abilities at hand. Overcoming obstacles means having to improvise a solution to a problem when you don't have what you want. Resilient people make the most of what they do have.

Message in Practice

Why do some messages fail, while others succeed? Let us look at some practical examples:

On 8th May 2017 the world awoke to a newly elected president in France. A new, but young president by the usual political standards. He was 39 years of age and interestingly enough, he was neither the favourite nor was he the best choice. In fact, you could say he was the negative choice.

Emmanuel Macron, unknown, an ex-banker and not necessarily a leader of choice. As the world watched in anticipation to see where this went, he ran his campaign against the far right European stalwart Marine Le Pen.

An interesting thing happened during this election.

- Le Pen had the better CV.
- She joined politics when she was elected regional councilor in 1986 and moved up the ranks.
- In 2011 and 2015 'Time 100' listed her on the top 100 most influential people in the world.

Macron on the other hand was an investment banker who only became active in politics in 2012 when he was appointed deputy secretary general under Francois Hollande.

During the election, there were tell-tales signs that things did not go according to plan. Some of the ballots were blank, about 8.5% and about 25% of registered voters did not vote.

Three questions need to be asked.

- Is the popular or obvious choice necessarily the leader that will be followed?
- Will this maybe open dialogue on how we choose to follow leaders in the future?
- Was there really no other candidate in the whole of France?

Why would you follow a certain leader?

A leader in business or politics needs followers; people that follow the message. If we look at the difference between a leader and a manager then one conclusion comes to the foreground, **a leader is the one with the message**.

We really don't know what the singular message was that Macron had, but people sure did not want to follow Le Pen's message. Should we please the people? Or should we stick to the message we have? One thing is certain, and that is that our message should inspire people.

Many leaders today have a message, but does it inspire you? Let's look at some of the big guns in politics:

- Barrack Obama: "Yes we can." Can you remember the opponent Mitt Romney's message? "Get America working again"
- Donald Trump: "Let's make America great again" can you remember Clinton's message? That she was uniquely qualified for the job
- Macron "Together France". Le Pen's message was "Choose France"

This is a political leader example but the point is not

whether it is politics or business, the point we are debating is the message. If you compare the message of these political leaders, what do you notice?

- Obama had a message of hope. He inspired the people to believe that is was possible to get America back on track. Romney on the other hand seemed to be insinuating that Americans were lazy.

- Trump, who is a successful businessman, also had a message that inspired. He suggested Americans should follow on the message of Obama and believe they could make America great again. After the 9-11 bombings and all the other setbacks, Americans needed to believe they could once again make America the super-power it used to be. Clinton on the other hand had no clear message and was simply trying to justify why she should have the job.

- Macron, also a businessman, suggested that unity for the French was the way forward. This was in contrast to Le Penn who suggested that the French choose France. They were French and were already in France, so what was there to choose?

Let's look at a business example. Remembering that Trump and Macron were successful businessmen before entering politics so their message would have evolved from their business background.

- Southwest Airlines "We carry passengers using planes" the other airlines used "We fly planes that carry passengers". This message focuses more on the customer than on the business goals, and therefore attracts the customers as they feel that this large corporate is there to serve them and not only the shareholders.

If you ask the voters in France, most of them reply with a "I can't vote for her". In other words, we will rather follow someone else - and why is that? - TRUST - people either trust your message or they don't.

Le Pen's message: "Choose France" did not work for her. Ask yourself why? The answer is that the French already live in France, therefore the message did not work because they had already chosen. "Together France "is not a great message, but it is the better alternative, the better narrative, in business today your customers, staff and suppliers need a message they can believe, a message they can trust. Leaders in the world of today need to build a consistent trust relationship. When you do not have that trust relationship people will start looking for direction in other places.

In a world where there is so much uncertainty, we as leaders need to look at our message, we have to live it, and we have to become the trustee of someone else's future. So, when you decide on your message or slogan for your business it must not be normal, average or mediocre.

Make it short, powerful and give it substance. When you tell your message, deliver it with conviction, passion and determination.

There are only two questions to ask yourself:

1. What is your message?
2. Who are you going to tell it to?

Many of us are employed in management positions but we don't realise that we have to do more than administrate and control, we need to lead.

Too often we want to lead by giving commands, order our followers to do something as opposed to taking our saplings and subordinates on a journey of discovery into the unknown. What is the unknown you may ask; tomorrow; the next quarter; the next year? Definitely not. The unknown is not tomorrow, but it is the journey you take to get to tomorrow. When you take a journey, there are many discoveries you make along the way, lessons you learn by yourself and from others along the way, and so much you can teach and show others.

Imagine driving along a beautiful countryside and suddenly you see a mountain rise up to the sky in front of you. You stop, get out and follow the footpath to the peak of the mountain, but someone else has been there before you; what would you find? Empty cans, or plastic bags some idiot who had no respect for the amazing beauty of the landscape dumped there? Someone who was there before you?

Now, imagine, you stop at the mountain and there is no way up the mountain, no footpath and the ascent seems utterly impossible. There was nobody on the mountain before you; no-one to blaze the trail and tread out an easy footpath to follow. How do you know the ascent will be impossible if you haven't even tried?

So, you put on your hiking boots and you decide you are going to climb that mountain no matter whether it seems impossible or not, and lo and behold, you find this untarnished beautiful panoramic view, this unsurpassed beauty, and those who follow you up there will join in your fulfilment.

Where do you get that dream? Making money is not a dream, it is the result of the achievements towards the vision and the vision is your dream. If your team buys into your vision they will start to follow you up the mountain that has no footpath.

So, what do you have to do to let them know what the dream is? Structure it into a motivational message. A leader without a message is not a leader, you become like a drill sergeant barking out orders and commands.

Get a message, live the message, become the message. Be the example of that message.

Do you believe your message? Are you passionate enough about your message to ignite the passion in your followers?

Mentorship

Mentoring can probably best be defined as a professional relationship in which an experienced person (the mentor) assists another (the mentee) in developing specific skills and knowledge that will enhance the less-experienced person's professional and personal growth. This gives better meaning to the term "taking someone under your wing."

The following are some of the functions that could be required from a mentor:

- Guiding the mentee about a specific topic or skill
- Guiding the mentee to master a particular skill
- Guiding the overall growth of a mentee by sharing resources and networks
- Challenging the mentee (applying pressure) to move beyond their comfort zone
- Creating a safe learning environment for taking risks and making mistakes (failures)
- Focusing on the mentee's total development in the designated area

A mentor may coach, but a coach is not a mentor. Mentoring is "relational," while coaching is "functional." There are other significant differences.

MENTORING	*COACHING*
Takes place outside of a manager-employee relationship, and is at the mutual consent of a mentor and the mentee	Managers coach all of their staff as a requirement of the job
Mentoring in general is career-focused and therefore focuses on professional development that may be outside a mentee's area of work	Coaching takes place within the confines of a formal manager-employee relationship
The relationship is personal as a mentor provides both professional and personal support	Coaching focuses on developing employees within their present jobs
The relationship may be initiated by a mentor or created through a match initiated by the company	The interest in coaching is functional, and is determined by the need to ensure that individuals can perform the tasks required to the best of their abilities
In mentoring, relationships often cross job boundaries	Relationships in coaching tends to be initiated and driven by the manager
Mentoring relationships usually last for a specific period (nine months to a year) in a formal programme (an informal mentoring relationship may continue)	Relationships in coaching are finite and end once the employee moves to another job

Your message is what drives you. It is your vision or those goals you have set yourself. As a business, you need to have an indication of where you are going, a business roadmap if you like.

If you do not know where you are headed how do you ever expect to convince anyone to follow you?

You need to know where you want to steer your business or team as a leader. There is no point in asking someone to follow you and when they ask you "To where", you don't know.

The formula elements for mentorship are as follows:

Mentor = Time x Pressure - Failure

- **Time** = Distance/Rate

MULTIPLY BY
- **Pressure** is defined as force per unit area

MINUS
- **Failure** is the inevitable result of an accumulation of poor thinking and poor choices

Time

Time, as a mathematical formula, refers to distance over speed. We have revised the formula slightly to refer to speed as the rate at which someone develops.

One can easily apply this formula to various situations in the work place, but in the case of mentoring a mentee, you need to carefully consider the distance a mentee travels in the progress of mentorship and at what rate they achieve the end result.

Let us consider a practical example from the workplace to test the formula. Tony was a waiter at an upmarket restaurant, but according to Tony he was not receiving the amount of money in tips during an evening that he had originally expected. Tony learned that he was in fact receiving tips that was far below the average tips per waiter. Tony was not happy with the situation and decided to investigate ways to improve his income from tips.

Tony enrolled in a practical waitering course to learn the skills of being an excellent waiter and identify the weaknesses in his waitering skills. Tony felt that by knowing what is required from a waiter and how a waiter should act would greatly improve his skills and then also increase his earning potential from tips.

Tony discovered that the skills and knowledge required by a successful waiter related to aspects such as understanding the functions of a waiter, serving techniques, hygiene factors, personal grooming and knowing the contents of the menu to enable the waiter to make suggestions to patrons.

On self-examination Tony realised that his nails were not always clean and neatly trimmed; his hair was at times unkempt and not properly combed; and his trousers were saggy and did not give a neat appearance.

Tony immediately decided to take action to improve these key areas. He did not have to learn how to do it as he already knew what to do he just had to apply it. This meant that Tony could complete the course much faster and therefore he shortened the rate of learning.

So, using Tony as an example we can see that the distance he needed to travel was that he needed to take a course that made him a more efficient waiter to stand a greater chance of receiving more tips in an evening.

The rate referred to the time Tony had to spend to complete the course. In the example used we can see that the time spent learning a new skill can be shortened if the subject learns faster and the rate is increased if the subject takes a longer period to develop the skill.

In Tony's case, the faster (rate) he developed new skills (distance) as a waiter the more productive he became and shortened the time spent with him as a mentor. This also then had the domino effect of improving the return on the investment in his training.

Pressure

Pressure is mathematically defined as force per unit area. Applying pressure (or energy) in a business environment we propose that this pressure is applied in two distinct ways.

The first way is the pressure we apply to increase the skills base of the employee and it that way expand their comfort zone.
The second way is by applying pressure to specific areas where the employee needs to focus attention for purposes of improvement.

Comfort Zone Pressure

If followers are committed to the task and they know exactly what to do but still do not do it, it could be that they have a problem with their self-image, a concept introduced by Ian Mann[1]. Self-image refers to what each person perceives their abilities to perform a specific task to be. Whatever you feel your ability is, that is what is known as your comfort zone.

If you ask someone to perform above their comfort zone, in other words you apply some pressure, they will feel uncomfortable with the task and revert back to their comfort zone thus not putting in the required effort as they feel that they cannot do that particular job well.

If you ask a person to perform below their comfort zone, they will feel that they are not doing well enough and as a result they will lift their performance to get back into their comfort zone.

The only way to get someone to perform better therefore is to increase their self-image. This is usually done through applying additional pressure and forcing them to try new things to increase their level of skills.

By increasing the pressure, you will get them to move their comfort zone higher.

Area Pressure

In the process of improving someone's skill levels, you will be required to focus on areas where there are shortcomings and "apply pressure" to those specific areas to ensure improvement. This requires that you zoom in on a particular area and pressurise the leader to develop the skill by either obtaining assistance or mentoring or even additional coaching.

The two areas identified for applying pressure could be combined when pressurising an incumbent leader to develop a certain skills or area of their overall leadership skills. The need to develop or hone the skill would be required for the potential leader to become a better leader but will also assist in stretching their comfort zone.

There is a school of thought that describes this pressure as giving the potential leader a mountain to climb that is very difficult. Then you make it almost impossible for them by moving up the time lines that they really struggle to accomplish the end goal.

Then before they fail, or you could even allow them to fail depending on what it is you want to achieve, you provide them with the resources to achieve the goal.

Another way of applying pressure is through setting goals. When setting goals, you should consider the following:

- **Set priorities** - When you have several goals, give each a priority. This helps you to avoid feeling overwhelmed by too many goals, and helps to direct your attention to the most important ones.

- **Write your goals down** - This has the effect of solidifying them and gives them more meaning.

- **Keep operational goals small** - Keep the low-level goals you are working towards small and achievable. If a goal is too large, then it can seem that you are not making progress towards it. Keeping goals small and incremental gives more opportunities for reward. Derive today's goals from larger ones.

- **Set performance goals, not outcome goals** - You should take care to set goals over which you have as much control as possible. There is nothing more disheartening than failing to achieve a personal goal for reasons beyond your control. In business, these could be bad business environments or unexpected effects of government policy. In sport, for example, these reasons could include poor judging, bad weather, injury, or just plain bad luck. If you base your goals on personal performance, then you can keep control over the achievement of your goals and draw satisfaction from them.

- **Set realistic goals** - It is important to set goals that you can achieve. All sorts of people (employers, parents, media, society) can set unrealistic goals for you. They will often do this in ignorance of your desires and ambitions. Alternatively, you may set goals that are too high, because you may not appreciate either the obstacles in the way, or understand quite how much skill you need to develop to achieve a particular level of performance

There are three major goal setting procedures:

- SMART goals which was first identified by Peter Drucker[2] in line with his concept of WBO Work Based Objectives where he states that goals you set should be Specific; Measurable; Achievable, Realistic and Time-Based. The concerns raised with this form of goal setting is that although goals are specific they may be set very low and therefore there is not sufficient pressure on the incumbent leader.

- Cascading goals that require the most senior executive, most likely the CEO to set goals in line with the company strategy and then each subordinate down the line sets their own goals in line with that of the CEO. The problem with this form of goal setting is that it takes an immense amount of time to eventually get down to the lowest level.

- Percentage Weighted goals where each action or element of the goal is afforded a weighting factor in order of priority or importance.

The concerns raised with this type of goal setting are that whoever is rating whether the goals are achieved may not understand the weighting system applied to the goals and therefore measuring whether the goals were achieved or not becomes opinionated.

In 2002, professors Edwin A. Locke and Gary P Latham[3] revealed the results of their 35 years of research on goal setting in an article for the American Psychology journal. The summarised results of their findings show the following:

- By setting specific and difficult goals will consistently lead to higher performance and is more effective than just urging people to do their best.

- Set tight deadlines as this will lead to a higher work pace and therefore the successful achievement of objectives and goals.

- Get public commitment from the person as this will ensure buy-in and will increase the personal commitment of the person.

- Locke and Latham found that it really makes no difference who sets the goals as the goals will be achieved based on the above criteria.

- The goals could be set by the individual, by mutual agreement or individually

- The goals could be set by the manager, team leader or the big boss

Let everyone know exactly what their goals are and the predictable result will be increased effort, greater persistence and better performance.

However, most leaders chose not to follow Locke and Latham's advice and persist with any of the top three methods of goal setting

A sensible approach would be to find a suitable blend of the various goal-setting techniques and apply them to achieve maximum results with your team.

Failure

Failure can be loosely defined as the inevitable result of an accumulation of poor thinking and poor choices. By not having the correct skills and not following the proper procedures it is easy to fail. It was Albert Einstein that said, "Someone who has not made a mistake has never tried something new."

As a leader, you need to apply the pressure to extended the person's comfort zone but you need to allow them to experiment with processes and their own ways of completing tasks, within the allowable procedures of the company of course, and have the freedom to make mistakes and fail.

Failure builds experience and also allows creative problem solving to take place. Through failure someone can learn lessons on how not to do things and discover the correct way of doing it.

Let us look at a few examples:

In developing a commercially viable light bulb, Thomas Edison actually went through over **ten thousand prototypes** before getting it right. That means he failed 10 000 times at the same job before he got it right. What would have happened to modern society if Edison had given up after failing 5 000 times? We would probably still be using candles.

From the experience that Edison gained through his failures, inventors have since been able to further the technology so that we have various light sources today.

- Henry Ford is today known for his innovative assembly line and American-made cars; but he wasn't an instant success. His early businesses failed and left him bankrupt five times before he founded the successful Ford Motor Company.

- Most people are familiar with this large department store chain called Macy's, however what very few people are aware of is that R.H. Macy started seven failed business before finally hitting big with his store in New York City.

- Most of us take Einstein's name as synonymous with genius, but he didn't always show such promise. Einstein did not speak until he was four and did not read until he was seven, causing his teachers and parents to think he was mentally handicapped, slow and anti-social. Eventually, he was expelled from school and was refused admittance to the Zurich Polytechnic School. He was labeled "addled" (unable to think clearly,

> sometimes confused) in school and therefore was educated at home by his mother, who was a teacher.

If your followers fail once in a while, just remember that they are in the company of some of the greatest leaders and thinkers of our time. Again, we want to emphasise that the defining criteria is that a person must learn from the mistakes made otherwise you are repeating the same mistakes and will never achieve the desired results.

Give your followers room to fail and to grow and you'll reap great rewards.

Here is an example of how true leaders should deal with setbacks and failures:

Two friends attended a classy black-tie function and, as it so often happens at these events, they soon got around to discussing the successes of their respective businesses. The one starts bragging about how much money he had made the past week. Not to be outdone, the other counters with a higher figure. As the drinks start to flow and the conversation becomes more heated, they start showing off their ability to exert power. As it would happen, both are in manufacturing and fitment of after-market parts for high-end off-road vehicles.

The first guy explains how he will be firing his senior technician the next day for causing an accident in the workplace that cost his company $100 000 in damages. As you can imagine, the conversation eventually escalated to a point about to how ruthless they got when procedures were not followed and how firmly they act and react to exert their authority.

Then another businessman, who was in more or less the same type business, upon hearing them bragging about ending this technician's career, decided to join in the conversation.

The original two bragged about their influence in the industry and how they belonged to all the various associations, and how they would close the doors for this technician so he would never work in the industry again. As you can imagine, with the bragging and showing off fuelled by the steady flow of alcohol, they were going to show who was in charge.

The third businessman, who had joined the conversation, politely enquired if he could get the contact details of the technician in question.

The businessman in whose employ the technician was at that point asked him: "Why would you want to contact him? Are you crazy to want to employ someone like that?" To which he replied: "Oh no sir, he has just had $100 00 worth of training and I could never let someone like that slip through my fingers."

Therefore, you will realise that a mentor has an important function to fulfil in the development of a mentee or follower. Being a mentor is a specialised role and it differs drastically from a coach, facilitator (trainer) and a manager.

Let us explore the meanings or functions of these various role-players.

- A trainer or facilitator is someone who teaches the incumbent or mentee a new skill by explaining mostly the theoretical content of the skill. They will use training manuals and visual aids to get the knowledge transfer to take place.

- A coach on the other hand is someone who works alongside the incumbent and ensures they can perform the skill that has been learnt in a practical fashion. They are there to correct any mistakes before or as they occur.

- Micro-managing, which is what most managers do when someone s learning a new skill, is where the manager may as well do the work themselves as they are so engrossed in the incumbent's tasks that they want to control every part of the action. Someone who micro-manages has control issues and in most cases, does not have the confidence in their own job so they attempt to be in control of everything that remotely relates to their jobs to ensure no-one can unset them in their position.

- Mentoring however, is neither of the above. Mentoring is a process where the mentor walks alongside the mentee. This does not need to take place literally, as the mentor could be distanced from the mentee but still offer support and guidance to the mentee.

Let's use a very simple but illustrative example of making a cup of coffee.

- The trainer or facilitator would teach the mentee about the various countries coffee is grown; and the types of coffee that could be produced with the various techniques.

- The coach would work alongside the mentee showing them the ways to actually make the cup of coffee and correct their actions as they progress through the stages of making a cup of coffee. The coach would typically use phrases such as "No, don't pour the water in yet, let it boil first" and so on.

- The micro-manager would basically make the coffee himself or supervise the mentee to death. Typically, a person that micro-manages would first want to check themselves if the water has boiled. They would also want to check that the correct amount of coffee etc. has been placed in the cup. Micro-managing could also goes as far as expecting the mentee to ask for permission before they pit anything in the cup.

- A mentor on the other hand would let the mentee make the cup of coffee and then afterwards, having tasted the coffee, tell the mentee that the coffee was nice but that it tasted a bit but bitter, for instance. The mentor would then not tell the mentee how to fix it but, because the role of the mentor is to develop the mentee, rather ask the mentee what they think they could do better next time to ensure the coffee is not so bitter.

Great leaders mentor and do not coach or micro-manage. Coaching and micro-management should not form part of the armoury of a mentor even though very often we combine the various roles into one and say we are mentoring. Instead a mentor should approach the mentoring process with an attitude of "let me join you on your road of discovery".

Great leaders become great because they too have mentors.

BE A CATALYST

What is a catalyst? The Merriam-Webster dictionary, as explained in the beginning of this book, describes a catalyst as an *"agent that promotes significant change or action"*. So then it stands to reason that if you intend on being a catalyst as a leader, you have to cause action or change. You have to get your followers to change the way they act, think, re-act and approach tasks or problems. You have to be an agent for change.

We have specifically devised the leadership formula that has been discussed previously to enable leaders to follow the simple process in order to achieve the end result. Along with the leadership formula a leader should:

- Have a message, believe the message with the utmost conviction and share the message
- Possess the attributes of the leadership flag and apply them to all situations both in the workplace and in their personal lives
- Display the desired level of leadership maturity which is described further on in this chapter

To illustrate what we mean by becoming a catalyst, let us look at Penny's story

When he left school, he was lost. He didn't know where he was going, he didn't know what he was doing. He didn't know anything about management or leadership. He didn't have a degree or a specialist direction and eventually started with the only work available to someone like him which was as a security guard.

His first day on the job the only message he received was "Here is a uniform, wear it with pride." He received no training, no induction, just the instructions "Don't let anyone through that is not on the list." What list, where is the list? To this day, he has still not seen that list.

When he got married 13 years ago, they were financial broke and were getting nowhere and were fighting to survive; fighting so hard to stay alive that they could barely afford to pay the instalments on the car they were driving.

There was a time when they were so broke, he could not even afford a new pair of shoes. The shoes had holes in the soles and he was really desperate. One day he had the opportunity to visit with a friend of his that had just purchased a carton of cigarettes. This friend was a heavy smoker, and because he smoked so much, soon one of the carton of cigarettes was empty. Penny immediately, being very resourceful, saw an opportunity to relieve his shoe problems. He took that carton paper from the pack that was empty and cut the cardboard out in the shape of the soles of his shoes. The fit was perfect and he placed the newly formed soles into his shoes and in that way managed to prevent his socks from damage and moisture for a while.

At that stage in his life, his wife and he had learned to eat cabbage, even though they were forced to eat it out of desperation, they came to love it. Today he can make cabbage with any meal, any a multitude of ways. You don't have any idea how many ways there are to cook cabbage. Ask Penny, he should know, by now he has become quite the specialist.

Until one day, a man named Peter came to him with a question. This man asked him: "What is your message". Penny was trying to survive 'till the end of the day, never mind the end of the week, or even the end of the month for that matter, what message was this man talking about? Talking and messages won't feed his wife and him, Penny mused. But the man told him to get a message and believe it, because that message will define the rest of his life.

That day Peter became Penny's catalyst. He took him under his wing and became his mentor. He taught him the theory of being a leader and a catalyst, but allowed him to make mistakes along the way in the practical application. The only precondition to allowing failure, was that there had to be a lesson that was learned through the failure. Penny could not simply make mistakes and chalk it up to experience as the experience only developed if he learned from the mistakes.

Many years later, Peter became a senior executive at a large listed company. He was a real leader.

Last year Penny and his wife were in the kitchen preparing a meal together. They had again bought a cabbage. As he cut the cabbage in half he automatically proceeded to cut out the core, that white hard bitter piece. His wife stopped him from discarding the core and asked him not to throw it away, but to cut it up, because his cocker spaniel loves that white hard piece of the cabbage. As Penny proceeded to cut the core into smaller pieces, he took a bite to taste it and it was hard and bitter.

The next week they bought another cabbage, this time Penny put the whole core into the pressure cooker and cooked it with some of the other leaves of the cabbage, and lo and behold it had a sweet soft taste.

In a very similar way companies go through a vicious cycle of hiring and firing people without ever dealing with the core of the problem. For lasting results, for building and maintaining an effective team time needs to be invested, we need to add energy with the right pressures and we need to allow for mistakes. When you do that, when you've become a catalyst leader then you can change the person that has become the hard bitter core in your organization.

LEADERSHIP MATURITY

The concept of leadership maturity is built on the backbone of Eric Berne's Transactional Analysis theories. The three stages are described showing how leaders mature by applying various skills and techniques in their leadership journey to enable them to become the effective catalyst required to affect change in the team.

Parent

A leader that displays the traits of a parent style leader, is a leader that demands results and inflicts punishment if the instructions are not carried out correctly. This form of leadership is manipulative in nature and does not get sustained results.

A parent style leader will be like a parent that will instruct a child to perform a task by enforcing their positional authority over the child and whether the child wants to perform the task or not is irrelevant as the child is fully aware that should they not obey the command, they will receive some form of punishment.

The parent enforces this type of obedience because they are in charge, they are the parent.

In exactly the same way a parent style leader will not take the opinions of the followers into account, but enforce the adherence to the command for the simple reason that they are in charge: and therefore, they consider themselves to have the power. There are times when this type of leadership is necessary such as in the military where the whole structure is designed to enforce the adherence to commands without hesitating or questioning the command. Unfortunately, in most business environments this will not solicit the desired result.

Child

A child leader is a manipulating leader who preys on the emotions and guilt feelings of the team members and followers.

In the same way, a child will throw a tantrum or use some psychological angle to manipulate the adult to give in to their demands, the child style leader will prey on the emotions of the follower and use manipulative guilt induced ways of ensuring the objectives are achieved.

A child is also quick to point out the shortcomings and faults of the parent, and in a similar way the child style leader will constantly highlight the faults and shortcomings of the team or followers to coerce obedience.

Adult

As adults, we have matured over years through experiences and life lessons learned. Adult style leaders are disciplined, realistic and considerate of the strengths and weaknesses of the team.

The adult leader will develop the team interaction to the point where there is proper motivation and the team members or followers are carrying out requests and instructions because they have the desire to do so. In the case of the parent style leader, followers are reacting out of fear of reprisal or punishment; even fear of losing the job. On the flipside, in the case of the child style leader, the followers or team members are reacting out of guilt or pity: they feel guilty that they are not doing a good job or do not have the proper skills and therefore they carry out the instructions; they feel sorry for the leader because their job is so tough and they seem not to be coping.

The desired leadership maturity type is therefore the adult style as this will ensure the proper cohesion of the team and there will be an atmosphere of camaraderie and mutual respect. This style of leadership will also assist in identifying and developing future leaders from within the ranks of the team.

In the formula $M^s \times nM^e = C^n$ the n refers to the duplication of the mentee and catalyst. What this implies is that as an effective leader you could mentor more than one mentee and this would then result in your being a catalyst to more than one mentee. It therefore stands to reason that if you have a clear message, you need to drive it with passion and conviction and not be swayed easily. In driving the message, you mentor your followers and team members (mentees) and the more mentees you have, the greater you become as a catalyst.

You must bear the following in mind. It is possible and advisable to be a mentor to more than one mentee at a time as this strengthens your team and your message, but you can only have one message or your formula would change to:

$$nMs \times Me = C$$

where the C now represents Confusion and not Catalyst (2 Messages mutiplied by Mentorship leads to Confusion). You cannot have mixed messages or more than one message.

Let us examine some leaders and see how they measure up against the Leadership Formula.

The Herbalife story begins in 2002 when then founder Mark Hughes passed away leaving his empire behind. The company should have folded but somehow stayed solvent. Michael O Johnson the former CEO of Walt Disney Pictures became the new CEO. Johnson was used to creating hype through movies and selling dreams and fantasies. However, Johnson's strength as CEO lay in the fact that he was a health and fitness fanatic who was now the CEO of a nutritional supplements empire.

In 2015 the **_Federal Trade Commission (FTC)_** of America launched an investigation into Herbalife. Even this could not slow the nutritional product empire down. About four months after the investigation was launched, Michael O Jackson resigned stating personal reasons as the reason. The FTC claimed that Herbalife was a criminal business that operated the same as a Ponzi or pyramid scheme.

Bill Ackman, a shrewd investor, using a mathematical formula he had developed, predicted that Herbalife shares would eventually be driven down as far as US$0. This prompted Ackman to institute a short position on Herbalife shares to the effect of US$1 billion. The shares of Herbalife have since see-sawed up and down, but mostly down, but have not yet reached US$0.

Ackman scrutinized the business model of Herbalife and realised that for the company to make money, it did not depend on the amount of turnover derived from direct sales, but Herbalife instead made money and paid the commissions from sales derived from a downline.

The day after the **Consumer News and Business Channel (CNBC)** report of the **Federal Trade Commission (FTC)** accusation, Ackman presented a "public short" the likes of which no one had ever seen before. A public short is a risky, fairly rare phenomenon in which an investor not only bets on a stock to go down—known as **short-selling**—but publicly announces that he has done so, explaining why. On this occasion Ackman delivered a 3½-hour, webcast lecture in which he called the company the "best-managed pyramid scheme in the history of the world."

He expected the stock not just to decline but to go to zero. He made it clear that if his bet paid off, he'd donate his personal profits to charity, because he considered any proceeds from a corporation so villainous to be "blood money."

By the following Monday, Christmas Eve, Herbalife stock had fallen 42%, from $41.57, where it had stood before Kelly's report, to a low of $24.24, with the company having shed close to $2 billion in market value.

So, how do these two leaders, who could both be deemed great leaders, measure up against the Leadership Formula?

COMPONENT OF FORMULA	MICHAEL O JOHNSON	BILL ACKMAN
Message – Conviction	Johnson had conviction of his message. He believed in the Herbalife concept because he was a fitness and health fanatic	Ackman was convinced that he had the correct prediction and that Herbalife shares would drop to zero. He is still driving that message with conviction.
Message – Passion	Johnson was passionate about his message because he was passionate about his fitness. He managed to build a strong business that was very successful	Ackman was so passionate about his message and that he would be successful, that he was prepared to bet other investors that he was correct

Note: The these comments and opinions are based on the information we were able to source through research conducted on the two individuals. Our attempts to secure interviews with them in an effort to verify this was unsuccessful and has meant that we formed our own opinions.

	MICHAEL O JOHNSON	**BILL ACKMAN**
Mentor – Energy	Because he did not invest any time in the possible mentees, there was clearly no energy spent	Because he did not invest any time in the possible mentees, there was clearly no energy spent
Mentor – Failure	Due to no time or energy being spent on mentees (distributors), no room was allowed for lessons to be learned from minor failures. This resulted in major failures occurring and created the constant loss of distributors. The business model is also doomed for failure in that there are not enough people in the world to successfully implement the model.	The process failed to deliver any followers as no mentees were initiated into the programme. There was failure and no lesson was learned, because if time and energy had been spent on prospective novice investors, they too could have developed some of the phenomenal skills Ackman possesses.

part 3

THE CORE OF THE CABBAGE™

WHAT IS THE CORE OF THE CABBAGE™

Following on from Penny's experiences with the cabbage, let us consider the principle of The Core of the Cabbage™. The concept of this principle was born from the "Peel the Onion" concept which refers to peeling away the layers of a problem until you have established the root of the problem.

Have you ever peeled away the layers of an onion? As you peel away layer for layer of the onion you are ultimately left with nothing.

Revisiting the story described in Part 2: The Leadership Formula, Penny decided to make an attempt to make the core edible but first he had to add energy to it. He had to process that hard, bitter core to change the way it was before. He put it into a pressure cooker along with some of the leaves and added some other agents (additives) to allow it to be converted into something that could be eaten and enjoyed.

In the world of today, we find that our company does not perform, our team does not deliver and we start peeling back the layers to see where we can get to the core of the problem. We peel back these layers one by one and right at core of it we find the problem or person which we realise is a hard, bitter core.

As is the normal practice in today's modern businesses, we don't want to handle the problem and therefore we are faced with the harsh reality that this hard and bitter core is out of place and we should get rid of it and that is usually our first reaction. When we are placed in a position where senior management consists of primarily Baby Boomers and the up-and-coming workforce and the junior executives are Millennials, this problem and situation is aggravated ten-fold due to a clash of values and character.

Let us look at a practical example that could be happening in any workplace at this very moment. You have an employee named James that works for your company and he does not perform according to the set standard of the company. He is negative and because of his constant unhappiness, he spreads that negativity inside and outside of the organisation, such as suppliers or customers, he comes into contact with. He is disruptive, he does not meet deadlines and is always late.

James has all the excuses in the world why he fails, and always blames someone else or everyone else for his failures. The natural and instinctive reaction of any manager or leader in current organisations would be that James doesn't fit with the corporate or business structure and would have to be fired because you just don't have the time or even the desire to deal with James anymore and the simplest solution to you is – cut out the core and discard it.

The problem with cutting out the core of the cabbage and

discarding it is that the next cabbage you get will still have the same hard, bitter core, and so the cycle keeps recurring and perpetuating itself as you employ, train, fire and employ, train and fire all over again. Do you see why certain organisations and even industries have such a high staff turnover?

What if we stopped there at the core and decided to do something real about it, something like adding energy to it? What if we became a catalyst, and changed the alignment of the atoms to make it better, softer, and sweet on the palette.

Let us look at an actual example from the workplace and see how we could apply this to the Core of the Cabbage™ and how someone could become a catalyst.

Peter worked as a sales manager for a large company that sold computers. James worked at the same company as a salesman. According to Peter, James was arrogant and very lazy and he had all the excuses in the book when he did not perform the way he was required to perform. He never made his sales targets, he was late for work and sometimes he was even rude to the customers.

Then one day, Peter called James to his office to discuss his behaviour and lack of work ethic. Peter asked James where he wanted to be in the future and how he saw his life transpiring at the current rate. Peter knew that everyone in life has a goal even if they express their goals in a tangible. Peter did not tell James what he had to do to make a success of his life, instead he started asking James a series of questions about his current situation, his life in general and where he planned to be in the next few years.

Peter wanted to get some insight into James' perspective on his own life. There were several issues that surfaced during this informal interview.

James had a girlfriend who was pregnant with their first child, and at that stage his personal life was in total disarray. He had no father who could provide him with advice and to give him guidance in life. This spilled over into the workplace as he had no-one at home to guide him how to act appropriately in the workplace. The result of this was that James was constantly in trouble at work and it was this continuous trouble he was in that eventually led to this discussion between him and Peter.

Peter decided to become James' mentor and started spending time with him setting objectives for his personal life and his career. Peter impressed upon James that he had to face the reality of his current situation, and had to admit that he was his own biggest failure, and not look to others for the reasons things were not working out. Even though he had been dealt some tough blows in life, it did not excuse him from taking responsibility for his own actions and ultimately his own future. The journey James had started out on actually had nothing to do with his work situation, but rather with his personal life.

One of the first things Peter did as a mentor was to teach James how to budget so that he could manage his finances properly, especially in the light of the new baby that would make its appearance soon. Once James had set a budget, he realised that he could not afford certain luxuries on his current salary. He had to manage his budget in a way that allowed him some additional disposable income which he could save in order to build up sufficient funds to afford these luxuries.

Peter also showed James that he had to realise that he needed to set personal goals as well as work related goals. It took James about a month to realise that he could actually change his future and that the power lay within him to do so.

The message Peter was trying hard to drive home with James was: "You decide your own future". Peter drove that message with conviction. In fact, Peter was so serious about the message, he lived the message with passion. Peter himself was going through personal problems of his own but he kept true to his message.

Every morning in the briefing session with the sales people, Peter would advocate the message with conviction and determination, even though he had personal problems at home. Nobody was aware that Peter was in fact having marital problems which were as a result of his situation having forced him to live in his mother-in-law's house with his wife.

In fact, for Peter to really be a catalyst for others, he had to drive his message home with conviction without his team knowing what personal problems he was experiencing. Although it is not humanly possible to leave your personal problems at the front door as you may have heard so many times before, it is important to realise that these problems do not magically disappear when you walk in to your place of work and then latch onto you again when you leave. However, if you want to become a catalyst and lead your people to believe in and follow our message, you must learn how to camouflage your personal problems so they do not interfere with your message.

As his mentor at work, Peter taught James the skills of the trade. Peter did not go easy on James because he had personal issues, but because he wanted James to grow and progress both at work and in his personal life, he set James impossible targets to see how he would perfom under pressure.

Peter kept on motivating James to show him that it was possible to achieve the targets and increase his comfort zone. Even though Peter drove the positivity issue to the point of exhaustion, Peter was determined to show James the way forward. Peter was convinced that he could be that catalyst that would get James to develop into a stronger salesman and also a stronger person.

The end result was that James started to motivate himself. He started to drive Peter's message, while he was still developing and honing his own message. That insurmountable mountain James had faced earlier had now become a molehill by comparison and James realised that he could climb that mountain one foot in front of the other.

When you become a mentor for someone, you have to allow for failure. James did not succeed at the first try. He messed up a big order, and the owner of the company wanted Peter to fire James. Because Peter was James' mentor at that stage Peter took James through the process of how to fix this mess. They did eventually lose the order, but the most important point about the whole process was that the lesson was learned.

Over the next six months James became the top performer

in the team. He started thinking outside the box, and James' arrogance changed to confidence, which eventually allowed James to excel in his job and in the process, he also became the top earner. James outgrew the company within next year and received other offers which Peter's company couldn't match.

At the end of the day Peter was the catalyst that realligned the atoms for James. James was the hard, bitter core of the cabbage who Peter should have fired on the spot. Instead what Peter did was become the catalyst for James to change to the point where, as the core of that cabbage, James became soft, palatable and tasted good to eat. The knock-on effect that occurred was that James' newfound confidence was so contagious, that it inspired the other sales people to also follow his example. So indirectly Peter actually became the catalyst for a number of people.

The main component that is required to make you a catalyst is to have a message. That message must be clear and you have to believe your message. If you do not believe whole-heartedly in your message, and live out your message with conviction, people will not trust you enough to follow you and adopt your message.

Your message could change over time as your goals change, but each message you have should become your focus, and you should drive the message with conviction.

WHAT IS YOUR MESSAGE

Your message is your vision. Your vision tells you where you are headed, where you want to be at a particular point in time. Your vison or message, as we have been pointing out throughout this piece, could be seen as your Final Destination

If you don't know where you are going, you simply won't know how to get there either. If you think that merely having a message is a quick fix to your problems, stop reading and start flipping burgers on the beach front, then you will have the opportunity to be on holiday and go nowhere.

You need to know what your message is but you also need to proclaim your message to your followers; otherwise your message is of no use, not even to you.

Mixed Messages

So, you started a new job, and you are looking to next month's salary, which will bring you the reward you have been hoping for, but you don't really know where you will be by then.

You then take on tasks which are given to you by your superior and work diligently to impress your bosses. Soon you start to realise that there are misunderstandings within the workplace that start to cause problems.

You experience some conflict at work and people don't necessarily like you. You might be popular at work, but the bosses are not that impressed with you. Sooner than you think, you will find that you are lost and don't know how you got to this point of feeling miserable.

The first thought that pops in your mind is "I need to move, I need to get my CV out there!" So, what went wrong?

A couple of questions spring to mind that could be applicable to your current situation

- Did you know what was expected of you in your job?

- Did you know what your role was in the bigger scheme of things?

- Did you perhaps have a job description?

- If you were lucky enough to have a job description, did you understand your job description?

- Were you properly trained or did you receive proper induction?

- Where you properly inducted in the company's vision, mission or objectives?

- Did you understand the culture of the company you work for?

Chances are that you have answered "NO" to at least one or more of these questions.

Many times, companies have a mission statement. Many times, they don't. The first thing you need to do when you join a company, is to find out which direction they are taking, where are they headed? Do they have a game plan?

Many companies have a brilliant mission statement. They give you documents and induction papers to sign. They take you on a tour.

The first thing they show you during induction, that is assuming they do actually induct new employees, is the reception. Guess what they show you next? The canteen or coffee bar on the premises. You are bombarded with hyperbolic statements, as the induction officer will ramble on, such as:

- "You have to taste our coffee, It's the best".
- "...it comes all the way from Kenya and is lightly roasted at precisely 205 degrees Celsius. "
- "You should taste our croissants, it is butter heaven!"

Many induction officers simply brag about the company they work for and tell you all the wonderful things the company has accomplished.

- "You must understand how well we are positioned in the market place"
- "We turned over 400 million last quarter"
- "We sponsor the annual fig festival"

Although it is important to know these cultures and accolades of the company you are joining, it still doesn't tell you where you fit into the bigger picture nor where the company is headed.

Sometimes you don't even have an induction officer because the company does not have any formal induction programme in place. You simply get handed over to the guy in the next office who is instructed by a line manager or the Human Resources Department to show you around. How is this going to assist you in knowing what your objectives are? How are you understanding the message of the company?

There could be a potential problem that arises because the person in the office next door has been instructed to show you the ropes. He might feel threatened by you and therefore develop a negative attitude towards you. He might come across as negative towards the company. Maybe he is one of those workers who is just waiting for Friday so that he can charge a glass and lift the elbow to a rough week and get lost in the moment of fake euphoria, called weekend.

You need your staff to work together as a team, so therefore socialising is important and team building is important. You want your team to have interpersonal relations and have an amicable atmosphere in the workplace, but getting the party animal of the company to present the induction programme might give the new employee the wrong impression of the bigger picture.

Would you really want the person who is just there to collect a pay cheque at the end of the month give induction to the new employee?

Would you really want the weekend alcoholic or party animal to be the ambassador of your company's future or brand? As a matter of fact, why not find the person who is the most negative person in the company to conduct the induction or introduction to the company, and see if this will get the new employee to resign before the end of the first week.

The overriding problem with all the participants in the induction scenarios mentioned is that they did not buy into the final destination or the message of the company. They don't understand where the company is headed. This is really important to get the new employee to a point during induction where they will understand that there is a final destination and what that destination is.

When they start their new career or new endeavour with the company, they should be able to have a clearly defined path towards the company's final destination.

There are some major points to consider when you conduct induction programmes:

- On the first day of the induction all the paperwork should be handled by the Human Resource Department.

- The induction should be carried out by a motivated person that has a career path aligned with the company's final destination

- This person should have a certain level of energy that is contagious.

When one works in a cubicle the whole day you seem to get negative quickly.

You must employ motivational steps to get the employees such as accountants, cubicle workers and other lone wolves on board and to get them to align themselves with the final destination.

DEFINING THE COORDINATES

Set the definitive coordinates regarding the direction your company is taking to prevent misunderstanding the end result. For years we conduct business as usual, we read reports, we set up goals and so forth, but do we ever stop and look at the big picture and where we currently fit into this picture?

It is going to take effort, a whole lot of effort, to turn a company into a new direction when you realize that it is already facing in the wrong direction. It is going to take more effort than you might be able to provide. Alone it would likely be an impossible task which is why mentorship, leadership, dealing with the core of the problem and getting clarity on where you need to go is so important.

Imagine your company as a ship and you are the captain of that ship. How will you as the ship's captain turn that ship around in the water on your own?

It is impossible! You will need the help of every crew

member to help; from your second in command, to the crew and you'll even need the help of the cook.

- The cook might be required to change the shift schedule,
- He might have to change the times he serves the meals,
- Maybe he has to change the entire meal type to be prepared.
- He might even physically be required on the deck to give a hand.

Let us look at some of the scenarios and how these scenarios might evolve.

The captain needs to change the direction of this sailing ship. It must happen now! It is a crisis! It is an all-hands-on-deck situation.

Everybody is required on deck in the emergency. Everyone's assistance is needed. As night approaches and everyone is completely focused on the emergency at hand, it turns late and night falls. The crew experience the one crisis after the other. Eventually it's midnight and the crew is tired, they are hungry and irritable.

The cook returns to the kitchen to face yet another dilemma. The cream has gone sour, the cheese has melted and the potatoes have turned black. What now? Eventually, to save the day he makes sandwiches for dinner for the entire crew. Eventually when the crew does go to bed, they are hungry and extremely irritable.

The ship has been turned around and is now facing in the right direction, but everybody, including the captain, goes to bed hungry and tired. Even the cook goes to bed hungry and tired.

The next morning the cook is so tired he oversleeps and wakes up late. He has now lost so much time that starts late with the preparation of breakfast. Because of the lack of sleep and the crises from the previous night, he is not able to perform at his optimum level, so he tries to remedy the situation and again serves only sandwiches in an attempt to deal with feeding the crew breakfast.

Now additional scenarios begin to evolve and further crises await the captain and the crew. Complaints begin to surface and everyone is unhappy. The mechanic feels he is the most important person on the ship, because he has to make sure everything is running smoothly and the engine must be fixed and in proper running condition at all times, so he complains to the rest of the crew and they start feeling negative.

What they do not realize, is that the captain has undergone the same fate as they did. He also had a sandwich for dinner last night, as it was the same case with the breakfast.

Now the head of the cleaning crew, who is just as grumpy joins in. He is also hungry and has very little energy to complete the tasks for the day on deck. He shouts at the deck-hands to clean up the mess that was caused by the other crew members. He trips over a rope and shouts at the rigger and demands that he picks up his tools and equipment from the deck.

Before you know it, the rigger turns around, grabs the head of the cleaning crew by the throat, the cleaning crew jumps in to assist the supervisor, because they will not be insulted, nor will they allow their supervisor to be assaulted by someone who looks down on them as cleaners. The rigger team decides that they will not stand by idly and watch one of their comrades being attacked, so they jump into this fight as well. Eventually the crew needs to break up a fight on deck. Everyone is annoyed with each other and the atmosphere is tense.

The crew then sends a party of representatives to the captain with the intention of having there say to resolve this issue that has transpired, and they will not be swayed. They don't knock, they simply throw open the door and the spokesperson opens his mouth and let's rip with the speech they have prepared, and what happens next, nobody expected.

The captain jumps up and shouts at his crew throwing all the rules of proper communication out the door. The captain, himself still hungry as well, and is just as irritated, is suddenly confronted by some low-ranking members, who have burst into his quarters without observing proper conduct and protocols. They have disrespected his privacy and his rank, he is the captain after all. He retaliates with an aggressive attitude because he has to show that he is still in charge of this ship. He has to assert his authority.

So where did the issue start out?

The captain had to change the direction of travel. He needed everyone at their positions. Everybody was called to help. The cook left everything he was busy which he wanted to serve for dinner on the counter, outside the fridge, in the heat left unattended because it was a matter of urgency. When the cook returned to the galley, the food had gone off.

If we view the situation from an objective perspective, we will notice that the cook got to the urgent, but forgot the important. He could have taken steps to preserve the food which would have led to the dinner being filling and well received.

IMPLEMENTING THE CORE OF THE CABBAGE™

When you want to implement the Core of the Cabbage™ concept in the workplace, you need to consider some factors.

There are two aspects that are important when important in applying this concept and they are things you need; and then there are thing you need to do.

The things you **need** would include:

- The leadership qualities that are defined in the Leadership Flag.

- Conviction and a strong belief in your values and message

The things you need **to do** include:

- Putting in the effort. You need to spend the time and you need to pay the price.

- You need to add energy by applying just the correct amount of pressure. Too much or too little pressure will result in not achieving the objectives.

- You need to allow for mistakes or failure - as long as there was a lesson learned. What is the price you pay today for training? is it worth it? Do we not spend too much on all these popular or accredited training programmes but the actual application in the workplace keeps on failing because we fire people too quickly, demote too fast, replace too soon, and not allow for the failure to take place in order for us to analyze it and learn the lesson from it?

- You need to apply the Leadership Formula
  1. Message X Mentorship = Catalyst
  2. Message = a passionate, goal chasing, determined and driven message of hope which is derived from your Vision
  3. Mentorship = Time X Energy - Failure

Let us examine a recent example of how things went wrong and how they could have re-energized the core.

On 8 September 2016, Wells Fargo bank announced that it would be paying US$185 million in penalty fees for creating fake accounts. The bank employees had created fake accounts, using fake email addresses and PIN numbers for customers, that the customers did not even know about.

The CEO John Stumpf claimed not to know anything about

it as "he was not an expert and knew nothing about these things" as he claimed during the congressional hearing. He was however the instigator of the whole debacle.

John Stumpf's message he preached to the bank employees was "8 is great." This implied that the employees of the bank were to push to have each customer of the bank have at least eight Wells Fargo bank products. This was an almost impossible target, and along with the incentivised sales programme that the CEO had implemented, employees figured out an ingenious way of creating these fake accounts to achieve the "8 is Great" targets set for them.

When the news hit the streets, Wells Fargo simply fired approximately 5300 employees who had been involved in the scandal. The bank, as mentioned was fined US$185 million, which was a drop in the bucket considering they had made over US$23 billion in profits (presumably mostly from the crooked scheme), and John Stumpf, the CEO, stood to get a payout of US$200 million if he should resign.

Not a good example of how to deal with the Core of the Cabbage™. What other options did they have available to them? Firing the 5300 employees is a typical action of removing and discarding the core. It is the easy way out but does not resolve the problem.

It is also a weak leadership quality as it implies passing the blame to someone else and not accepting the responsibility or being accountable for the team's action because you hold the role of leader. John Stumpf's declaration to the congressional committee that he was not an expert, is synonymous with sticking your head in the sand and hoping

the problem would disappear. A sort of Ostrich Management style. What should have happened? How could they have energized and re-worked the core to make it acceptable?
By accepting responsibility for their actions, and by realizing they were accountable to the customers and public, they could have salvaged part of their reputation. The trust relationship had been broken and this would result in the loss of customers and future business for the bank.

Instead of denying responsibility and passing the blame, they should have conducted a thorough investigation to determine how exactly the activity had started and how it was possible to not be detected through the controls in place. As the employees were showing their own warped sense of loyalty to the bank by attempting to fulfill the wishes of the CEO and reach the 8 is great target, they should not merely have been fired.

By investigating their motives behind the actions, some of them could possibly have been acting out of sheer desire to perform and be recognized.

With the correct mentoring and intervention, they could be re-energized to be a continued asset to the bank. Instead they appeared to become the scape-goats. By admitting their faults and announcing a clean-up and restructuring of the controls and administrative systems, the bank could have regained some of their credibility and the trust of the customers. Instead they chose to cover it up and pass the blame, thereby merely cutting out the core and discarding it.

Wells Fargo bank has since 1 January 2017 done away with the incentive scheme that caused the scandal in the first place instead of re-energizing it and making it work.

A cheaper and more productive option would simply have been to keep the existing staff. A study[1] conducted in 2012 indicated that there were astronomical costs involved in replacing employees. These costs ranged from loss of production, training new replacements and so forth. The study estimated that the costs (based on an average of the 3 groups identified) could be around US$40 000 per employee.

If we take the 5300 employees that Wells Fargo fired and multiply this by the average cost of US$40 000 per employee, we have a staggering figure of US$212 million just replace them. This amount is more than the fine that was paid by Wells Fargo and also more than the payout Stumpf would receive if he resigned. The total impact on the bottom-line would therefore be in excess of US$400 million. That seems to be a rather large core to discard.

The example above has negative connotations due to the Core of the Cabbage™ not being implemented. Let us also look at a positive example of how this actually works:

Herb Kelleher of Southwest Airlines is a prime example of how to apply the Leadership Formula and the Core of the Cabbage™.
Herb Kelleher claims that 'the business of business is people." A classic example of this is demonstrated in the following case study.

In a **World Of Business Ideas (WOBI)** broadcast in 2016, Herb Kelleher recounted an incident where one of Southwest Airlines' probationary employees sent him a letter regarding his message. In the letter, she questioned Kelleher as to whether he believed his own message. The message he was driving was that Southwest did not set rules, but instead they gave guidelines which in turn allowed their employees to use their initiative. The letter explained that due to extreme weather conditions, no flights could get out of Baltimore. What this employee then did was to hire five busses that carried the passengers from Baltimore to Long Island. Southwest gave her an award for using her initiative.

Let us now dissect this story by firstly measuring it against the Leadership Formula:

- **Message:** The message Kelleher and Southwest were driving was clear; we have set guidelines not rules. They drove the message with conviction. Because they believed their message and drove it with conviction the employees also believed the message and therefore followed the message and vision of Southwest. The employee was determined to follow the message to the point where she put her job on the line to implement the message.

- **Mentor:** Inadvertently Kelleher was a mentor for the probationary employee because he allowed her to use her initiative and possibly also make mistakes. He invested a lot of time in driving his message to the point where his employees believed in his message and put it into practice. He applied energy and pressure to allow the employee to use her initiative even though she thought she could lose her job. The pressure allowed her to make the decision because she believed that Kelleher believed his own message.

- Kelleher therefore is a Catalyst Leader as he was able to successfully drive his message and mentor his employees (Message X Mentor = Catalyst)

Now let's investigate how the Core of the Cabbage™ has been applied to the same incident. The crux of the Core of the Cabbage™ is to peel away the leaves of the cabbage until we encounter the core.

The situation that unfolded was that the weather had deteriorated in Baltimore to a point where it was not possible for the planes to take-off. By peeling away the leaves the probationary employee discovered some known facts.

Firstly, passengers needed to reach their destinations and secondly the weather was so bad that no planes could take off. The core was identified as the passengers that were stranded in Baltimore airport and they needed to get to Long Island.

She could have cut the core out and discarded it by simply sitting back and declaring that she could do nothing about the weather so the passengers would have to sit out the storm and wait until the planes could take off again. Instead she decided to re-energize the core and change its characteristics so that it became acceptable.

How did she re-energize the core? She realized that the passengers needed to get to their final destinations and that waiting for the weather to clear was not the solution, nor was it driving the message of the company which declared Southwest's commitment to its passengers by becoming the "most loved, most flown and most profitable airline," along with their mission to be dedicated to the highest quality of customer service.

Customers would not believe that you are committed to high quality customer service by simply leaving them stranded at Baltimore airport.

The guidelines instead of rules as proclaimed by Kelleher required employees to use their initiative. For this reason, she hired five busses to transport the passengers to their destinations. Even though this incurred additional costs for the company, she so strongly believed the message Kelleher was driving, that she was prepared to take the initiative and resolve the passengers' problem.

The examples used in Part 1 through Part 3 prove that to be a Catalyst Leader, you must firstly pledge allegiance to the Leadership Flag; you must apply all the components of the Leadership Formula in your role as leader and to be successful you must re-energize the core of the cabbage and not simply discard it.

153

CONCLUSION

CONCLUSION

This is not your standard conclusion of a book. We have explained the three concepts in the book at length namely; the Leadership Flag, the Leadership Formula and the Core of the Cabbage™. We have summarised each concept at the end of each part to help you come to a clear conclusion. In the same way, we have tested the Leadership Formula against some of the top leaders of our time. Now is the time to test it against your own leadership style.

You must now write your own conclusion. To assist you with writing your own conclusion, we have included the following assignments for you to complete as you develop your leadership skills and move another step closer to becoming a Catalyst Leader.

Assignment 1:

Do some research and identify three possible mentors you could work alongside. Research the message they drive. How convicted are they of their own message?

Do you believe their message? Now select any ONE of these possible mentors and explain why you chose them as your mentor.

MY MENTOR

Assignment 2:

Identify and select five possible mentees and list them below. Make an appointment with each of these selected mentees and determine exactly what it is you can mentor them in.

MY MENTEES

1.

2.

3.

4.

5.

Assignment 3:

Now that you have identified the five mentees you plan to mentor and established their mentoring needs, what message will you carry across? Apply the Leadership Formula to your message and mentoring of the five mentees.

Assignment 4:

Using the results from the Leadership Flag exercise at the end of Part 1, complete your Leadership Flag on the next page by indicating what your actual scores were in the "Present Score" column. You must now consider where your gaps for development are and indicate exactly what development needs to take place to close these gaps and enter them in the column marked "Future Actions".

	PRESENT SCORE	FUTURE ACTIONS
LIFESTYLE		
EXAMPLE		
AUTHORITY		
DISCIPLINE		
EMOTIONAL INTELLIGENT		
REASONABLE		
SINCERE		
HUMBLE		
INFORMATION		
PASSION		

Assignment 5:

Identify five unsolvable issues in your workplace or your personal life and then use the Core of the Cabbage™ theory to solve these issues.

- Are these issues important and in line with the vision or message? If not, then discard the issue.

- Identify the core of the issue and describe how you will apply energy to the core to make it acceptable and still apply to the message.

- List the steps taken to re-energize the core to make it acceptable.

<table>
<tr><td></td></tr>
<tr><td></td></tr>
<tr><td></td></tr>
<tr><td></td></tr>
<tr><td></td></tr>
<tr><td></td></tr>
<tr><td></td></tr>
<tr><td></td></tr>
<tr><td></td></tr>
<tr><td></td></tr>
<tr><td></td></tr>
<tr><td></td></tr>
</table>

LEADERSHIP FLAG PLEDGE

Now that you have worked through this book and completed the attached assignments, we would like to introduce you to the Wave-Crest Leadership Flag pledge. All incumbent leaders that complete the Wave-Crest Leadership Programme take this pledge as part of their development programme. Having completed this book and the assignments we believe that you are on your way to becoming and effective Catalyst Leader and would therefore suggest that you commit to the principles of the Leadership Flag by taking this pledge.

WAVE-CREST
LEADERSHIP FLAG PLEDGE

I pledge allegiance to the Wave-Crest Leadership Flag as my core values. I promise to live a **LIFESTYLE** suited to a Catalyst Leader by being an **EXAMPLE** to all who follow me. I promise to lead with **AUTHORITY**, and to be truthful and **DISCIPLINED** in all my actions in an **EMOTIONALLY INTELLIGENT** manner. I promise to be **REASONABLE** by showing empathy and allowing for failures while still being **SINCERE** and **HUMBLE** in everything I do. I promise to get a message and share the vision and message through providing **INFORMATION** with clarity, yet to never stop learning,

Above all, I promise to drive the message with **PASSION** and identify mentees to duplicate my message.

Signed:____

Date: ____________________________

BIBLIOGRAPHY

Introduction

1. Yaverbaum, E. 2004. Leadership secrets of the world's most successful CEO's. Dearborn Publishing. Chicago
2. Maxwell, JC. 2011. 5 Levels of Leadership. Center Street Publishing. New York
3. Heath, M. 2010. Leadership Secrets. Harper-Collins. London
4. Taylor, FW. 1911. The Principles of Scientific Management. Harper & Brothers. New York
5. Berson, AS; Stieglitz, RG. 2013. Leadership Conversations. Jossey-Bass.
6. Peter, Laurence J.; Hull, Raymond. 1969. The Peter Principle: Why Things Always Go Wrong. William Morrow and Company. New York.
7. Adams, B. 2008. The Everything Leadership Book. Adams Media. Massachusetts

Part 1

1. Willink, Jocko; Babin, Leif . 2016. Extreme Ownership. Macmillan Publishers.
2. Mann, I. 2010. Managing with Intent. Zebra Press Cape Town
3. Goleman, Daniel. 1995. Emotional Intelligence: Why It Can Matter More Than IQ. Bantam Books. New York
4. Bennet, William J. 1995. The Moral Compass. Simon and Schuster. New York
5. Greenleaf, Robert. 1970. An essay on "The servant as a leader"
6. Maxwell, JC. 2011. 5 Levels of Leadership. Center Street Publishing. New York

Part 2

1. Mann, I. 2010. Managing with Intent. Zebra Press. Cape Town
2. Drucker, Peter F. 1954. The Practice of Management. Harper Collins Publishers. New York
3. Locke Edwin, A; Latham Gary P. 1990. A Theory of Goal Setting and Task Performance. Prentice-Hall. New York

Part 3

1. Boushey, Heather, Glynn, Sarah. J. 2012. There are significant business costs for replacing employees. Center for American Progress.

PENNY DU TOIT

Penny du Toit is the co-founder of the Wave-Crest Leadership Centre where young and upcoming entrepreneurs are groomed into becoming Catalyst Leaders. He co-authored the book **"Why Great Leaders are Catalysts"** and helped establish the principles of The Leadership Flag and the Core of the Cabbage™.

Mr du Toit is a business strategist and growth advisory expert with over 20 years of experience in the areas of risk, change and Catalyst Leadership.

In 2017 he spoke on Why Great Leaders are Catalysts at TEDxSwakopmund. He is a Catalyst Leadership trainer for companies and is a member of the Professional Speakers Association of Namibia, which forms part of the Global Speakers Federation.

Dr Rowan van Dyk holds a Doctorate in Business Administration and is a Leadership Catalyst trainer. Dr van Dyk has over 30 years experience in the field of management consulting and leadership training with training centrers in South Africa and Namibia. He has been contracted by the Namibian Training Authority to develop new outcomes based qualifications for Wholesale and Retail Trade.

Rowan is a founding member of the Wave-Crest Leadership Centre. He co-authored the book **"Why Great Leaders are Catalysts"** and helped establish the principles of The Leadership Formula, The Leadership Flag and the Core of the Cabbage™. Dr van Dyk is part of Toastmasters Swakopmund which forms part of Toastmasters International.